# A City Owned

# A City Owned

Murder By Increments Book 1

*O.J. Modjeska*

Copyright (C) 2019 O.J. Modjeska
Layout design and Copyright (C) 2019 Next Chapter
Published 2019 by Reality Plus – A Next Chapter Imprint
Cover art by Cover Mint
All rights reserved. No part of this book may be reproduced or transmitted in any form or by any means, electronic or mechanical, including photocopying, recording, or by any information storage and retrieval system, without the author's permission.

# About the Author

OJ Modjeska is a historian, criminologist, and author. She graduated from the University of Sydney with a PhD in Modern American History in 2004, and received her Graduate Diploma in Criminology from Sydney Law School in 2015. In 2015 she was awarded the JH McClemens Memorial Prize by Sydney Law School for her scholarship in criminology. Before pursuing a writing career she worked for many years as a legal writer and editor. OJ writes books of narrative non-fiction true crime and disaster analysis. Her debut, "Gone: Catastrophe in Paradise", about the Tenerife air disaster, is an ebook bestseller. "A City Owned" and "Killing Cousins" make up the two-part true crime series "Murder by Increments", now available at all good ebook retailers. If you enjoy this book and would like to receive news of new releases, consider subscribing to OJ's mailing list at the link below.

http://ojmodjeska.blogspot.com.au

www.estoire.co

# Publication Details

First published in 2018 by Estoire
Text © OJ Modjeska (Obelia Modjeska), 2018
This book is copyright. Apart from any use permitted under the Copyright Act 1968 and subsequent amendments, no part may be reproduced, stored in a retrieval system or transmitted by any means or process whatsoever without the prior written permission of the author.
Every attempt has been made to locate the copyright holders for material quoted in this book. Any person or organisation that may have been overlooked or misattributed may contact the publishers.

*In these caves I've dwelled for long*
*The lust for blood keeps me strong*
*Fly at dusk, land at dawn*
*Evil and darkness I bring upon*
*It makes no difference in my eyes*
*If I slay for right or wrong*
*Self-inflicted are their cries*
*In the graveyards they belong*
—The Circle of Evil by Atahan Tolunay

# Foreword

The criminal case dating from the late seventies which is the subject of this text is well-known, arguably even notorious. The perpetrators are familiar faces from the serial killer hall of fame. Nonetheless, I have deliberately omitted direct mention of them, or the popular name of the landmark case with which they are associated, until well into the narrative.

The reason for this will become clear to the reader in time. The celebrity of the murderers concerned should not detract from the fact that many significant details of the case are unknown, or have been forgotten—and recalling those facts from the vantage point of the present casts our understanding of the events in a rather new light. Indeed, journeying through this tale without any assumptions may deliver an experience far more contemporary and familiar than one otherwise might be expecting.

I wrote *Murder by Increments* after coming across some of the more obscure details of the case during studies for my criminology accreditation. At the time, I was stunned by the fact that—despite thinking I already knew what the case was about—I actually knew very little, and the facts I was learning brought to mind many of the horrors and sufferings that seem to be occurring with greater frequency in our present world.

As vile as the actions of the perpetrators were, almost as shocking were many of the responses of the police, the courts, and the psychiatrists to whom justice was entrusted. The criminal figures at the center of the story, in my view, are not its most arresting feature; instead, they were catalysts that through their actions revealed the frailties of human nature, and the outlines of a society tormented by itself. The suffering continues.

# PART ONE
# PANIC

# Chapter 1

This story begins in a vast and pulsing metropolis, the central districts of which are today noted for cleanliness, even blandness. It is a world of high-rise glass and steel, of functional if dull design. With its collection of music stores, the Rock Walk featuring concrete handprints of rock 'n' roll luminaries, and the historic Sunset Grill made famous by the Don Henley song of the same name, it presents a thoroughly digestible version of hip to the many tourists who flock to the city every year. The principle attractions are dining, shopping and scanning the surrounds for a celebrity or a dog in a tote bag. Nobody worries about visiting at night. It does not have time for crime, or squalor. This is no stomping ground for the marginal and deviant. Those folk have mostly moved on—to somewhere, anywhere, some other place; it doesn't matter.

Twenty odd years ago, Hugh Grant was very publicly arrested after receiving a blowjob from streetwalker Divine Brown in the front of his BMW. That was just before the big clean-up: large swathes of Hollywood were commercialized and purged of "undesirables". But native Los Angelenos who have lived in the city their whole lives will tell you the late seventies and eighties gave us Hollywood at its grotty worst.

Back then, the entire stretch of Sunset between Gardner and Western Avenue was a teeming sexual marketplace. Hollywood's east side thronged with pushers, panderers, bums and runaways. A porn cinema stood on the site of every old theatre. The detritus of the failed counterculture, drug casualties in bandannas and flared denim, migrated south from Haight Ashbury, their ideals dying gracelessly in the salty marinade of sex and drugs for profit. It was an interstitial time and place; the glamor and the production houses had gone

## A City Owned

elsewhere, the future and its juggernaut of cleansing commercial interests had not yet arrived, and in the empty space garbage collected in a steamy pile.

Hollywood circa 1977, when this story begins, was home of the desperate and damned. Any night or day of the week, cars would cruise the Boulevard, just slow enough for their occupants to size up the human wares lining the grubby pavements. The war between the cops and prostitutes simmered night after night, occasionally boiling over, then cooling off again. Right next to the Rocky and Bullwinkle statue on Sunset the city line dividing West Hollywood from the City of Los Angeles runs right through the strip. If a Hollywood cop car passed through, the women would move over to the West Hollywood side; if it was a sheriff's car they saw, they would move to the LA side. Most women preferred that side. The sheriffs were known to line the girls up against their vehicles and have them place their hands on the hood, then rap them over the knuckles with their metal flashlights.

Hollywood girls made dodging the cops into an art form. Most knew, for instance, that vice officers had Sunday and Monday off, so those were good nights to work. Some were known to call in at the station and if there was no answer, out they went on the job.

Sometimes though, no matter how clever you were, what precautions you took, you were going to get got.

The cops could go undercover, and pretend to be johns offering a job. Then, to make matters more confusing, civilian men posing as undercover police officers was oddly not an unusual situation.

Maybe it was just a sign of the times, the perversity of the modern world, but there was another kind of craze in town apart from disco dancing. In its basic form it appeared as guys screeching down Sunset, fake sirens attached to their vehicles, screaming abuse at the hussies. Scratching the surface there was something larger and more complex going on; something approximating a subculture. The visibility of trade in fake police paraphernalia and the numbers of men who drove cars made deliberately to look like cop vehicles pointed to the existence of a class of police buffs of various shades. Markets and swap meets sold fake badges, sirens, handcuffs, cop-style ID wallets and batons. There was also a black trade in the "real" things that had been misappropriated from the force, which could be acquired for a much higher price.

Some of these "buffs" were just young guys who liked to acquire an old police vehicle for its speed and good handling. Others took things more seriously.

These were men who liked to stalk crime scenes and pretend they had some legitimate business being there. They would install scanners in their cars and listen in on police calls. They might enjoy stopping motorists and hassling them about their inappropriate driving. Or they enjoyed harassing and intimidating prostitutes, pretending to offer a job and then flipping a badge just to see the look on the lady's face.

Their motivations varied. Some just did it for a laugh. Some were embittered police rejects. Some felt somehow impotent in their lives and enjoyed the feeling of authority that passing themselves off as a cop gave them.

The problem was you couldn't tell who was who. Many were perfectly harmless; some were dangerous beyond a woman's darkest imagining.

* * *

Tall, black and leggy, Yolanda took in as much as three-hundred dollars a night—in seventies money, a small fortune. After dropping out of high school she had spent a while waiting tables and washing dishes, doing what she was supposed to, respectable work for those with limited prospects. She barely made enough money to feed herself and her kid. Some of Yolanda's friends were hooking. She tried it, and handed in her notice at the restaurant shortly after. Fuck that.

Yolanda loved the money she was making on the game. She was a young woman in the prime of life, who enjoyed fashion and took pride in the way she dressed. She liked the things the good money she was making on the streets bought her: fine, sexy clothes. Nice jewelry, like her turquoise ring, set in a silver leaf clasp. She was no slob. She looked high end, more like an escort than a streetwalker.

It was just a job. She didn't plan to stay in it forever—a temporary situation, she told herself. It felt good to have enough money coming in to buy what she wanted for herself and her kid. But the job had a major downside—and there were a few, like the fact that she had already been booked for soliciting and had a criminal record at twenty-two. Gradually her whole lifestyle changed, she started using and moved in with a local pusher, and then the kid went to live with her grandmother. So she had become separated from her daughter, who had been the reason for going on the game in the first place.

On the night of 17 October 1977 these things were playing on her mind as she stepped out and headed to her beat. She wasn't feeling it and she missed her kid. In no kind of mood, she just wanted to get out there, do it, get her money and go home again.

She met her pimp along Sunset and he must have picked up her lack of enthusiasm, because he told her to haul ass and get out there before he got mad. He watched her walk off eastbound towards the intersection of Sunset and Detroit.

Ronald LaMieux ran an organ retailer in the music district of Sunset, near that same intersection. On the evening of 17 October, he and a colleague stayed late working to deadline on some auditing. At some point he was distracted by the sounds of shouting outside. He looked out the windows and saw what appeared to be a vice arrest of a tall, black prostitute happening on the street right out the front of his store. A man with dark hair and a mustache was waving a badge at the young lady and yelling.

LaMieux saw the man handcuff the woman and put her in the back of the vehicle. There was another man sitting in front in the driver's seat. Vice arrests of streetwalkers were common in that area of Sunset, and LaMieux didn't think much of it, except that the arresting officer seemed to have an unnecessarily aggressive manner.

Yolanda, sitting in handcuffs in the back of the car, was cursing her luck. Getting written up again was the last thing she needed. The cop who had arrested her, a young guy with a mustache and acne scars on his neck, told her they were going to take her down to the station, and then he had gotten into the backseat and was sitting next to her, which she thought was a bit odd. But it wasn't until she stared a little harder at the man driving the vehicle that she first sensed that something weird was going on.

She realized she knew the driver, or at least, she had met him before. He was older than the other one, with a big, hooked nose and bushy black hair, streaked with grey. Rather ugly, really. But there was something about him, Yolanda thought. She had thought so that day she first saw him. She couldn't make out his whole face, only his profile, but she was positive this was the same guy.

A few weeks earlier she had gone with her friend Deborah on an errand to see this man at his shop on Colorado Street in Glendale. He was an auto upholsterer. The place was full of foam and reels of thread and there was a sewing machine at a workbench. There were some very flash cars parked in the garage, a Merc and a Cadillac limo. The man had boasted that Frank Sinatra was one of his clients.

A face kind of like oily old leather, and that big nose—and yet Yolanda had felt strangely drawn to him. He had spoken with a soft voice, smiled in a barely-there way that just crinkled the corners of his eyes, and exuded an aura of unforced confidence. During their conversation she found herself mentioning that she could usually be found on Sunset around Highland.

Yolanda couldn't get the full details out of her friend, but she thought Deborah was selling the guy a trick list, a dossier of warm leads on johns. So he was an auto upholsterer and maybe a part-time pimp. And now here he was, a cop. This was when Yolanda started to think something was wrong.

—What's going on? You guys aren't cops are you?

The younger guy, next to her in the back seat, gave her a sharp look.

She kicked the back of the driver's seat with her high-heel.

—Hey! I know you. I've seen you before. You ain't a cop. Where are you taking me?

The driver turned briefly, and Yolanda saw his eyes. It was definitely the same guy; but his eyes were so different to the day she had spoken to him at his shop. The irises black, floating in the whites. Wordlessly they chastised her; for kicking the back of the seat, maybe just for existing. He looked angry as shit.

Shut up, the younger guy said.

And then it happened, so quickly that Yolanda didn't even see it coming; his fist landing hard on the side of her face.

And then she knew that something was really, really wrong.

These guys weren't officers, she didn't know who or what they were, but this was some game, some kind of bad trip, and she was going to hurt, she was going to get messed up real bad.

# Chapter 2

On the morning of 18 October 1977 a group of LAPD officers stood near the entrance to the Forest Lawn Memorial Park cemetery in Glendale, where Hollywood greats rest in themed divisions called Inspiration Slope, Slumberland, Sweet Memories and Dawn of Tomorrow, surrounded by replica Michelangelo statues. Its founder, San Francisco businessman Dr. Hubert Eaton, thought normal cemeteries were ugly and depressing, and wanted to create one with a more optimistic vibe, something more in line with the needs of Hollywood. Tacky or not, Humphrey Bogart, Walt Disney, Errol Flynn and more recently Michael Jackson have all paid vast sums to be buried there.

The cause of this gathering of officers of the law was the naked, lifeless body of a young woman laying on a grass strip by the side of Forest Lawn Memorial Drive.

Someone floated the theory that the killer was making some kind of ironic statement by leaving her there. Certainly her resting place, and the apparent manner of her passing, could not be more in contrast with the grandiose vision of death behind the gates. Completely bare, face-down, the rough splay of her legs and the way her arms jutted out at sharp, unnatural angles, seemed to suggest she had been—quite literally—dumped on the ground.

Above them the drone of cars whizzing by on the Ventura Freeway bled into the gentle hum of insects. A few feet from the body, a "no loitering" sign rose up out of the dirt.

After examining the ground around, the detectives came to a different conclusion. They stood at the top of the slope and followed it down to where she lay with their eyes. Disturbance to the grass and shrubs seemed to suggest the body had been thrown from a vehicle up on the freeway. It had rolled down the slope, coming to rest near the side of the road. The location wasn't important; it was simply where she had landed after being thrown from a car, like the wrapper of a McDonald's cheeseburger.

There was only one thing left on the body: a torn rag around her neck, possibly from her own clothing, the same that she had obviously been strangled with. Turning her over, the officers immediately saw the deep indented rings around her throat: clear, sharp lines telling of a killer who had used great force, and a death of extreme suffering. The eyes were florid with petechiae, broken blood vessels.

Who was she? Where had she come from? They had so little go on. Any clothing, jewelry, or possessions that might help identify her, that may gather fragments to connect her to her killer, had been stripped away. She was like a baby exposed on a hill. She could have been anyone, from anywhere. And if she had been dumped from the freeway, they noted, she might not have even been from Los Angeles, let alone the neighborhood in which they were standing.

A tossed body always presents difficulties. A body left at the crime scene almost always has something on it or near it to connect it to the killer. In this situation there was nothing.

The coroner's investigator checked for the approximate time of death by taking the ground temperature, then inserting a probe into the body in order to gauge the temperature of the liver. After death, the body temperature falls towards the temperature of the surroundings at a rate of about one-and-a-half degrees per hour. The detectives estimated that this young woman had died late the evening before, probably between ten o'clock and midnight.

They followed the usual procedure, dividing the area into a grid that was painstakingly swept for evidence. But the officers' gut instincts had told them this search would be fruitless, and they were right. Everything that was found had been there before the body was dumped. A door-to-door in the immediate area to find out if anyone knew the victim, or had seen anything suspicious, yielded no information.

If it was her job that killed her, it was also the only thing that permitted Yolanda to be identified at all. She had a prior record of arrest for soliciting, so her fingerprints matched records held in the county's files.

Later, the autopsy would find semen traces that came from two different men inside the body. Obviously it could not be determined that even one of these deposits had come from the same individual that killed her. According to analysis of the samples however, one of the men was what is known as a "non-secretor", that is, a person whose blood type cannot be determined from seminal fluid.

The officers didn't put much thought into considering the implications of these findings, or any others from the case. Once the mystery of Yolanda's identity was solved, they lost all interest.

Prostitutes turned up dead in Los Angeles all the time. As it was, there were too many homicides to solve already. The gang wars were in ascension and the decade was rolling towards an end which would see Los Angeles unofficially declared the murder capital of the world, and the morgues several days behind in processing bodies.

As for whores, murder was a collateral risk of the profession—a john gets too rough, there's a conflict over payment, and next thing you know, *bam*: dead. The common-sense view was that if they wanted to stay safe, they shouldn't have been doing it in the first place.

Case unofficially closed.

The wisdom of devoting little to no police resources to the murder of prostitutes of course rested on the assumption that men who killed whores probably weren't a threat to the mainstream community.

\* \* \*

Yolanda's murder was never reported, so the first her friend Lois heard of it was when some of her girls, wide eyed and trembling, told her that Yolanda had been found strangled to death outside the cemetery next to the Ventura Freeway.

Lois considered them her girls in the sense that they were both her charges and her subjects. She was a sex trafficking researcher, and also ran CAT, the California Trollops Association, an advocacy organization that provided social programs and legal assistance for prostitutes.

She was an oddity in Hollywood, wandering around with her pen and notebook, observing the local life as if it were native fauna. At least, she began that way. In 1976 Lee enrolled in a PhD program in sociology, and she was preparing her dissertation focusing on street prostitution in Los Angeles.

When she began, her path forward seemed clear. She would submit to the requirements of her discipline, remain neutral and scientific, gather data for the benefit of various agencies, document the subculture, write up the results.

As time passed, things got murky. She was getting too close to her subjects. Lee began to ask herself if her future lay in research or advocacy.

For her, the streetwalkers of Hollywood were not just prostitutes, but flesh and blood women. She grew to know them and love them like you would a sister, a mother or a friend. And the closer she drew, and the more they let her into their world, the angrier she got on their behalf. There was no justice at all for the women when they were subjected to violence and even death at the hands of johns and pimps. That anger spilled over again when Yolanda was killed, and the police showed little to no interest in finding out who was responsible.

Lee thought Yolanda's murderer might have been a pimp. Then again, if that was the case, there was probably some other motive. What had happened to Yolanda was so savage, so very brutal. Prostitutes were certainly casualties of pimp wars in Los Angeles, but it was more likely that they would get roughed up or have a couple of bones broken to send a message that it was time to move to another beat. Killing them was excessive and didn't really make sense. The girls were product, a source of livelihood. Even if the product belonged to someone else, destroying it was kind of an egregious transgression of professional ethics, and inviting more trouble than it was worth.

Even if the police didn't care who killed Yolanda, Lee certainly did. She didn't want any more women hurt or killed by the mystery perp. Deciding to take positive action, she went to talk with a dick she knew in the LAPD.

The officer was polite but firm.

—Miss Lee, we are snowed under here! This case can't be given higher priority than all the other homicides we're dealing with.

Lois curled her lip at the officer. She knew what that meant. That was just code for "we aren't interested in investigating."

It was always the same: the brutality and harassment the cops inflicted on the girls—tolerated without question up above—was bad enough. When crimes were perpetrated against prostitutes, they just didn't care. The prostitute was a criminal, not a victim.

Lois knew it wouldn't occur to them that these women usually started on the game when they were no older than their own daughters, that many of them had been raped and beaten by their own fathers, so it was a good deal, really—an improvement in their fortunes—to be compensated. Or, as she put it, they didn't have to lay in the bed and wait for daddy to come in anymore, they could take control of the sexual abuse and be paid for it.

She tried badgering the detective a bit longer, but he stonewalled her and she slunk away, stewing in cynicism and resentment.

The police weren't inclined to be helpful to her anyway. She had been researching thousands of police reports filed against prostitutes which were resulting in court challenges against the LAPD. The suits were for not arresting the male customers who paid the prostitutes, and focusing their efforts largely on women. The standard police approach to prostitution in the seventies—which would persist, astonishingly, for the next four decades—consisted almost solely of making street-level arrests of prostitutes, chucking them in the slammer overnight, and adding another misdemeanor to their record. The johns, even if occasionally caught and embarrassed, rarely encountered any real penalties, and pimps were barely ever caught and prosecuted.

Lee's legal challenges to the police were certainly radical for the time—but mostly, they were a nuisance. The LAPD thought she was a pain in the ass.

# Chapter 3

30 October 1977 was an ordinary night at the Fish n' Chips, a humble café famed deservedly or not for authentic British style fast food. Gathered around one scratched table was a collection of the usual low-hanging Hollywood riff raff, drinking coffee and idly swapping tales of woe.

Youngblood had had a bad day, but maybe no worse than usual. He woke late, and had managed to get into a fight before his first meal. This clown that owed him money had been blowing him off for weeks with lame excuses, so he had no compunctions about throwing down and destroying the guy's elbow.

That had provided a momentary release of tension, but did not solve the immediate problem of his lack of funds, so Youngblood was still ticked off about it hours later. He didn't have a profession as such. He was more the take-what-was-going type. If asked, he described himself as a disc jockey or a bounty hunter. If jobs were coming his way, they were usually in that line of work. But he had been floating all over America, following his whim, sometimes a woman, sometimes a job. He landed in Los Angeles, and lately, he hadn't had much work, or much money.

He bought Judy Miller a coffee anyway. At fifteen years of age, five-feet-two inches and only eighty pounds, he feared she might disappear altogether if she didn't get something to eat or drink.

Judy wouldn't have called herself a prostitute. Turning a trick was something she did occasionally for food or a few dollars. It was a matter of survival, not livelihood. If guys didn't have money to pay her, she often gave it away for free. The Hollywood of the late 1970s was still caught up in the free love philosophy of the hippie era. Only now it had taken on a grubby, less elevated tenor.

On the other hand, Judy was lonely, and sometimes she just wanted to feel close to someone. There was nothing in her past to suggest she was entitled to any form of security or any sense of belonging. Judy's family were dirt poor and couldn't afford the luxury of worrying about a kid that was almost an adult. She ditched school, ran away, and like so many others before her, was seduced by Hollywood's false promises. She didn't find money, fame or even a job. What she did find was people she could relate to, people like herself, people as lost and damaged as she was.

Judy's life was shit. This was actually the best she'd ever had it.

So when Youngblood suggested he might fancy a roll in the hay, even if he couldn't pay her, she went happily with him back to his rundown hotel, The Gilbert on Wilcox.

Afterwards, he felt bad. Not guilty in the sense that he had done something wrong, but because Judy really needed money. She needed food. She was barely surviving. It was brought home to him as he watched her dress, counting the ribs in her back. She didn't even have a full set of underwear. He threw a bra at her; an old girlfriend had left it behind.

Judy was a dolorous, plain girl, with lank red hair and a long, thin face that only accented the enormous size of her eyes. She was not one he would follow across the country, but he cared for her in his way. Youngblood told Judy he would take her out for a bite to eat.

The two ambled down Sunset, a mismatched pair, her so diminutive, he tall and broad, declaiming his hard edges in his leather vest and greasy blonde ponytail. In Carney's Diner, a restaurant converted from a rail car on Sunset, Judy demolished a hot dog.

—I gotta find a john, she said.

—Are ya sure? I'll get you another one. It's good huh?

Judy looked down and pursed her lips.

—I gotta go. I gotta find a john.

Youngblood's mouth was full of his own hotdog. He put his hands up in a silent gesture of defeat. Judy walked out.

From the diner, he watched her hovering at a spot in the parking lot. He felt sorry for her, just standing there alone in the dark, so small and frail, like the wind would blow her away at any moment.

But it wasn't long until somebody came. Youngblood saw him through the window of the big dark blue car; a guy with bushy hair and a big nose. He was dark-eyed, olive skinned. Maybe Puerto Rican, maybe Italian.

Judy talked to the guy through the window for a while, then walked around to the passenger side and got in the car. Youngblood watched as it motored away down Sunset, turned south and disappeared down the hill.

He felt better after that. He wiped the crumbs from the hotdog off his stubble and went home, and didn't think about Judy again for a while.

\* \* \*

On the morning of Halloween, 31 October, Chuck Koehn walked out the front door of his home on Alta Terrace Drive in La Crescenta, in the hills north of Glendale, and got into his car. Koehn's bracing daily routine saw him leave home at four each morning to work at his electrical shop. He would return home to shower and eat breakfast at about six o'clock, before resuming the day's work.

As Koehn pulled out from the curb and quietly made his way down the street, it was still pitch dark. Had it been lighter, he might have seen the dead girl lying naked on a flowerbed near the curb, outside 2833 Alta Terrace Drive. As it was, she lay undisturbed until his return at six, when the dawn light illuminated a pale, unmistakeably human form by the side of the road.

Koehn stopped his car and refocused his eyes, making sure he was seeing what he thought he was.

It was real. A tiny, naked girl splayed on the ground in the shrubs, right by the side of the road.

Koehn did not yet know that the girl was dead. Passed out drunk? An OD victim? Either way it was utterly surreal. La Crescenta was a middle-class, family neighborhood on the northeast border of the county, far from the vice and degeneration that had gripped central Los Angeles in recent years. People moved there to get away from stuff like this.

He got out of his car and walked over to take a closer look. His stomach lurched as he sighted the deep rings around her neck, the blue tinge of her skin.

This girl was dead. This girl had been murdered.

With hands that shook clumsily over the instruments, Koehn parked his car and went around to the back yard of his house where he retrieved a tarpaulin, returned to the body site, and threw it over the dead girl.

*A City Owned*

\* \* \*

A seasoned homicide detective with the Sherriff's Department headed a team out to La Crescenta after a caller dialled into the station, blathering about a naked dead girl by the side of a suburban road.

The guy was real worked up.

—She's just layin' there, he mumbled, his voice cracking. Just a few yards from my house!

Frank had been working homicide for several years, after transferring from major violations. He had done his penance to get where he was, completing the compulsory stint as a corrections officer assigned to all aspiring sheriffs, then landing a rookie post at the East Los Angeles station—the toughest in LA—and eventually rising to the rank of sergeant with the narcotics division at East Los Angeles.

But what he had always really wanted to be was a homicide detective. That, to him, was where the real action was. The nectar of justice. Meaningful toil. And he was known as one of the best. His was a relentless, grinding sort of energy, propelled by inquisitiveness and fondness for procedure. There was nothing flash about him.

He didn't know it yet, but he was about to become the most famous homicide cop in Los Angeles.

\* \* \*

Koehn was a regular sort of joe in Frank's estimation. He didn't throw up any red flags. Still, you couldn't really be sure these days.

—Detective Frank Salerno, he said, shaking Koehn's hand. You put this here?

He stared down at the tarp covering an indistinct mass on the ground.

—Yeah, said Koehn, all twitchy; what was I supposed to do? There are women and kids around here, kids getting up for school.

—It's okay …

Privately, Salerno was disappointed. By covering the body with the tarp, Koehn had potentially contaminated the crime scene. But Salerno could certainly understand him doing so. The guy was freaked out. This was far outside the realm of his experience.

Nice guy, family guy. His first instinct upon seeing the body had been to get it out of sight.

Frank gingerly lifted the tarp, trying to prevent the loss of any evidence. When he looked down at the victim, he knew right away that this was not a normal murder, whatever that meant. Not a murder committed in service of some other aim, or a means to an end. This was a killing in which the experience itself was likely part of the motive.

The strangulation marks that ringed her neck were deep and clear, showing great force had been applied. The fact that there were several marks around her neck suggested the possibility that the killer had taken his time, allowing her to revive several times before the final extinguishment of life.

Fainter marks around her wrists and ankles suggested she had been bound or manacled for her ordeal.

Nasty way to go. Real nasty.

She couldn't have been more than sixteen years of age or much more than ninety pounds. Her legs were spread apart, knees raised slightly, her arms bent out at an angle and her hands tucked underneath her.

The positioning of the body looked obscene, like the dead girl had been readied for intercourse.

* * *

The conclusion that the body had been lewdly posed on purpose was one reached by some members of the press who gathered on Alta Terrace Drive that morning to get the scoop on the bizarre finding of a dead, naked teenager on a suburban street. They read an obvious sexual motive into the crime scene.

Jim Mitchell, an investigative and general-assignment reporter for KFWB Radio, arrived at the scene without any previous briefing on the situation, apart from the fact that a female murder victim had been found. Mitchell—like Salerno—was about to make his mark in the world due to his involvement with a landmark case. His coverage would play a fundamental role in bringing the murders to the attention of the public.

Mitchell was well versed in covering homicides, and had seen more than a few dead bodies in his time. He stared at the dead girl, and silently mouthed the words: *what the fuck*. She was just lying there, naked, in a narrow parkway, surrounded by suburban houses.

There was something almost sacrificial, religious about the entire image. Looking down at the body he was struck by the way one's eyes were first drawn to her pubis, and the arms spread almost in a gesture of supplication.

He had never, in all his experience, seen anything like it.
He turned to one of the officers.
—Suppose it could be some kind of psycho?
—Uh, yeah, said the cop drily.
When Salerno looked at the positioning of the body, his mind, with its forensic conditioning, moved in a different direction. The girl looked like she had been deliberately posed like that. But it was much more likely that the body had fallen onto the ground in that position, because it had been dropped by two people: one carrying the girl by her arms, the other with his hooked under her legs. Her hands had caught under her as she hit the ground. There were no drag marks on the body, nor on the ice plant that covered the curb. This told Salerno that two individuals had dumped the body.

Something else made him think there were two people involved. A portion of the ice plant, opposite the victim's feet, had been disturbed, folded back away from the curb. Salerno thought maybe one of the men, carrying the girl's legs, had pushed the plant back with his feet.

He asked Koehn if he remembered if the ice plant had been bent like that the previous day. Koehn was confident it hadn't been. Woulda noticed that, he said. He and his neighbors were the house-proud sort.

Leaning in closer, Salerno noticed something very small on the victim's eyelid. A piece of fluff; some kind of fiber. Its significance as yet was a mystery, but in line with regular procedure, he removed it with a set of tweezers and bagged it as evidence.

Later, as he reflected on the day, he concluded that the thing that most disturbed him about the scene was what he guessed had Charles Koehn so rattled. And if it was your own neighborhood, you sure would be rattled.

Alta Terrace Drive was a cul-de-sac at one end, the other joining with La Crescenta Boulevard. Just a little higher up the hill was thickly wooded and dim, an ideal place to hide a body if you wanted to.

The killer, or killers, had made no effort to hide the body. They had wanted it to be found. They had wanted to scare people.

# Chapter 4

Days passed, and nobody reported the girl missing. A notice was placed in the *Herald Examiner* with an artist's sketch, in hopes somebody would come forward with information. Nobody did.

Meanwhile the coroner's investigation indicated that the victim had been strangled to death at around midnight, some six hours or so before she was found.

She had been raped and sodomized. Traces of an adhesive were found on the girl's face, indicating the use of a tape as a gag. All this underlined the possibility of an attack by a sexual sadist, by some kind of "psycho" on the loose, as Mitchell had put it.

But there remained the possibility that this victim, like Yolanda, was a prostitute, and the evidence of gagging and binding was part of a consensual sex game between her and a john, and the girl had been killed for unrelated reasons. Bondage was hardly an unusual request made of prostitutes. There was no sense at this time that the two cases were related, despite the similarities of MO. They were being handled by separate units. But the thinking about this case amongst detectives was, at the early stages, moving in the same direction: the victim was a street person who had fallen foul of her chosen lifestyle.

Salerno thought it likely that since nobody had come forward to assist in the identification, the victim was a runaway, one of the many drawn to Hollywood each year. Her youth and starved condition suggested the same conclusion. They arrived in an endless stream, usually escaping some sort of abusive or desperate situation at home, searching for something—fame or wealth, significance—and invariably found that nobody gave a damn about them or their problems. From there, the inevitable slide into crime, drugs, prostitution.

Judy's parents may not have come forward because they were far away, in another county or even state. Perhaps they weren't looking for her. Perhaps she had no parents.

So, following his nose, Salerno went down to Hollywood Boulevard after hours, in his civvies, and began showing the artist's sketch to the locals. The kinds of people Salerno was hoping to extract information from were addicts, pushers, bikers and prostitutes: not the most forthcoming with police. A man much like Charles Koehn, a father of three boys who liked football and fishing, he didn't care to spend his free time mingling with the denizens of Hollywood, but cracking a case was all about developing trust and rapport with witnesses; so out he went, always speaking to folks respectfully, maintaining a dialed down approach. In his favour, his presentation hardly screamed "cop". Bespectacled, with thoughtful eyes, a vaguely patrician bearing, and dressed in dorky sport casuals, he could have instead passed for a teacher or a librarian. His "witnesses" probably mistook him for a tourist who had got lost in the wrong part of town.

He kept hearing the same name: Judy. They said she was a runaway, just like he thought. A couple of them mentioned this Judy often hung out at the Fish n' Chips restaurant on the Boulevard. Salerno headed there next.

At a table in the corner sat a big meaty guy with a stringy blonde ponytail. Tattoos, denim jacket with the arms torn off. On the streets they called him Youngblood, but he gave the detective his real name: Markust Camden.

He nodded when shown the picture.

—Yeah, I seen her. Right here, a few days, maybe a week ago. What's this all about?

Salerno explained that if this was the same girl, she was dead—murdered in fact—whilst omitting as many details as possible. He wanted Markust to walk him through exactly what happened the last time he saw her.

Markust's eyes widened almost imperceptibly when he heard this news. Then he was straight back to poker face.

—Well, not much. Let's see, it was Monday. There was a group of us sitting right there at that table. I bought her a coffee. She left around nine or ten. That was it.

To Salerno, Camden seemed cagey. And he had an edge of barely concealed nervousness about him. But Frank's gut told him this was the type of witness he placed in a particular category: probably not directly involved, but not one-hundred percent truthful either.

The reason for that was Camden's eyes. They were tinged with fear, worry, maybe a kind of existential dread. This was a sad man, a feeling man. Judy's killer struck him as a very different type: someone cold, calculating. Lacking in fear.

Salerno sincerely doubted that this was the guy, but he also felt that maybe he knew more than he was telling. He gave him his card and asked him to call him if he thought of anything else.

Camden, of course, had every reason to be cagey. If Judy had been murdered that night after he had sex with her, that would probably make him a suspect. With all the dramas he had in his life, he didn't need one more.

\* \* \*

After more evenings scouring the streets of Hollywood for information, Salerno was finally able to track down Judy Miller's parents. They were not far away; camped out, in fact, at the Hollywood Vine, a rundown hotel in the old theatre district, practically a stone's throw from the Fish n' Chips. Despite her proximity, Judy had not cared to return home, and they had apparently not cared to find her.

The family of four—Judy's mother and father, and two little boys—were living in a single room littered with spoiled food and dirty diapers. A stench of sour milk, mold and feces hung in the air.

Given that their living conditions resembled a middle-eastern war zone, Salerno was not so surprised at their impassive response to the news of their daughter's death. Mr. Miller just nodded.

A father of three boys himself, Frank could never grasp how parents could be unmoved when something so terrible happened to their child. But it was easy to be judgmental from a position of privilege. Life for the Millers was obviously easy come, easy go. Judy's absence from their lives, and now her death, meant they had one less mouth to feed.

Mr. Miller identified Judy from the coroner's pictures, which for Salerno was the only positive from the whole encounter. The identity of the victim was now known, and that part of his job was done. In truth, he hoped he would never again have to dwell again upon the wretched life and death of Judith Lynn Miller.

Salerno had reasonable cause for such optimism. No immediate connection was drawn between the earlier murder victim found near the cemetery and this one. A somewhat competitive and antagonistic atmosphere prevailed over relations between the Sheriff's Department and the LAPD, and even if they had cared to compare notes on cases, information sharing was not a strong point. Sheriff's detectives tended to look down on the LAPD officers, who did not need to submit to the same rigorous standards of training and experience. Salerno's baptism of fire working as a jail warden for his first year was the baseline requirement for all sheriffs. The LAPD resented this impugning of their status, and countered that their officers had better street nous to manage tough crime. The divide fostered by these schoolyard squabbles meant that collaboration to solve cases crossing jurisdictions was a tall order.

In any case, even if the police had recognized the links in MO between the murders, taken as a whole—amongst the many homicides perpetrated against street people—they would still have appeared to be random events. Such people tended to come to untimely and vicious ends at the very hands of the company they kept, and nothing was deemed too unusual about it.

All those assumptions, however, were about to unravel.

# Chapter 5

Lissa was a professional dancer, but waitressing was how she had been paying the bills while she muddled through a strange, transitional period in her life.

She had spent much of the last year feeling under the weather, and for the time being, she wasn't rehearsing or performing with the LA Knockers. They were a distinctly weird local dance troupe that matched camp, outlandish disco fashions and moves with cabaret comedy. "Comic gags and shiny glutes", as a newspaper review called it.

Lissa had formed the group with girlfriends and fellow dancers Jennifer Stace and Yana Nirvana. They were increasingly popular at the clubs around Los Angeles, and Lissa was both proud and a little wistful watching their growing success. But dancers had to be fit and trim, and Lissa had recently developed hypoglycemia and put on weight. Adequate sleep and careful nutrition had been her priorities of late, and soon she would be starting anew, flying to San Francisco where she had been admitted to a performing arts school. All told, Los Angeles hadn't been doing it for her lately. She expected the change of scene in San Francisco and a return to meaningful pursuits would give her a much-needed boost.

On 5 November Lissa was finishing up her shift waitressing at the Healthfaire Restaurant on Vine, one of the many trendy vegetarian eateries that had sprung up around LA in recent years.

She planned on getting home quickly. In a couple of days she was catching her flight, and she still had to pack and clear out her apartment. Nothing was on her mind that night except the fact that she was dog tired, and she had a lot to do. She got into her green Beetle and drove off Vine onto Highland, turned right at Franklin, and continued on towards the Hollywood Freeway underpass.

Somewhere along Franklin she became vaguely aware that what looked like a cop car, white on the top and dark on the bottom, was travelling behind her. It was at some distance though, and these were well-worn roadways, so Lissa didn't think she was being tailed.

She turned into Argyle Avenue—and the car followed right behind her. At the junction of Dix Street, near her apartment block, she noticed the cop car flashing its beams. She pulled up and turned off the ignition.

As Lissa gathered up her handbag and some items from the car, two uniformed officers approached in the darkness. One of them fixed the glare of his flashlight on her through the driver side window, and with a slight wave of his index finger, motioned for her to roll it down.

—Police officers, ma'am. License please.

Lissa couldn't quite make out the man's face with the beam of his torch in her eyes. She squinted as she rummaged in her purse for her license, wondering what she had done to get pulled over. When she found it she gave it to the man, who now kindly averted his flashlight from her face and turned it on the license, inspecting it thoughtfully.

She now saw that he was a young man, probably in his mid-twenties. Short dark hair and a mustache. He had stereotypically handsome, if slightly sharp, features, marred only by a cluster of very visible acne scars around his neck and lower cheeks. Intensely blue eyes.

Lissa demanded to know what this was all about. She hadn't done anything wrong. She was a good driver. She was pretty sure she never ran a red light or anything like that.

But the man ignored her question entirely, as if she had never spoken at all. He just passed the license to the other one, the older man. He was rough looking, about as ugly as the other one was handsome, with a curly black shock of hair.

The older guy peered at Lissa's license under his flashlight. Then the two glanced at each other, as if exchanging some silent assent.

—Step out of the car please, said the younger one, quiet but firm.

Lissa objected. They had to tell her what the hell this was all about. This was a bunch of crap! She hadn't done anything wrong.

—We ask the questions, ma'am. But since you asked so politely, there's been some trouble over near Vine and Highland. A robbery. Your car was seen leaving the scene.

Lissa, aghast, struggled to explain: that was where she worked, she had just left her waitressing job over at the Healthfaire right now, she sure as hell didn't have anything to do with no robbery, and she was in a hurry to get home because she had a plane to catch.

The young cop pleasantly assured her that they would call her manager and straighten everything out. But in the meantime she was going to have to accompany them to the police station.

Lissa didn't see that she had much choice but to do what the cop asked. She could either stay put with them hanging outside her window all night, or get out. But something was telling her not to.

The young one told her to drop her bag on the ground, pushed her against the side of her car, and frisked her while the old cop started rifling through her bag. Now, perhaps a measure of her growing alarm, Lissa acquiescently told the men that she would happily accompany them to the station, but it wouldn't do them any good because she had nothing to tell.

—Be quiet, said the younger one. Stop making a scene. You'll wake up the neighborhood, and you're only making things worse for yourself.

His voice was low, but he was getting angry. Lissa noticed something weird about his eyes. The glittering blue of them, now, perhaps due to a deprivation of light internal or external, were black.

They bundled her into the back of their black and white "patrol car", closed the door behind her, and nobody ever saw her alive again.

\* \* \*

The next evening, the manager of the Healthfaire Restaurant headed in to work and opened for business as usual.

He was a little concerned when Lissa didn't arrive for the start of her shift. She was very conscientious, and would have called in if she were sick or was going to be late for some reason.

As the hours passed, with no sign of Lissa and no word from her, this mild unease grew into worry. He put a call through to Lissa's home number, which went unanswered, and then to Lissa's father, Bernard Kastin, who was listed as the emergency contact on her employment record.

Bernard thought the manager was right to be concerned. But he also questioned whether Lissa had skipped out on the job because she would be leaving LA soon anyway, even if that really was not like her. Maybe she was short on time with her preparations for San Francisco.

He decided to head over to Lissa's apartment. As he was driving to the complex, he heard a news report on the radio about the body of a young woman found in Glendale.

The woman was described as in her twenties, with long curly dark hair. A sick feeling came over Bernard. His gut told him that his daughter was dead, but his mind pushed it away. Everything would be fine, he told himself. It was just a coincidence. That girl they found, she just looked similar to his daughter, but his daughter would be alive and well when he got to the apartment.

There, the building manager buzzed Bernard in.

The bed was made. An open suitcase, partly packed for her flight to San Francisco, was on the floor. It looked like she had never been home the night before.

Now in a full-blown panic, Bernard Kastin called the Glendale Police Department and spoke with Dave O'Connor from the homicide division. He explained that he had heard a description of a body found in Glendale on the radio that sounded like his daughter, and that Lissa had gone missing. Bernard provided enough details about Lissa's physical appearance that the police thought it a reasonable likelihood that this was the girl they had found.

O'Connor brought Bernard Kastin to the morgue, where a closed-circuit camera had been set up, so identification of bodies would be less traumatic for the relatives of victims.

Bernard didn't want to look at the screen, but he did immediately, his eyes drawn there without his permission. There was Lissa. Her dark hair falling in large curls over her shoulders, the way it always did. The familiar shape of her slightly roman nose, the gentle rise of her cheeks. But her lips were a narrow pale smudge, the eyes tastefully shut so as not to betray their total lack of animation, and then, clearly, the deep dark blue rings around her neck.

So strange. Lissa, and yet not Lissa.

O'Connor didn't even need Bernard to confirm the identification. All composure deserting him, he collapsed in wracking sobs.

\* \* \*

Lissa Kastin's body had been found by a jogger next to the golf grounds of the Chevy Chase Country Club in Glendale. The jogger's eye caught something unusual at the bottom of a ravine rolling away from the side of Chevy Chase Drive. Peering down he saw a clearly dead naked woman lying against a guy wire that marked the borders of the golf course at the bottom of the slope.

Now, a completely different police unit again would be processing the scene.

The detectives from the Glendale PD quickly formed the view that the body had most likely been dropped from Chevy Chase Drive, and had rolled downhill. There was a three-foot guard rail blocking the road from the ravine. Near the golf course fence at the bottom of the embankment there was a deep drainage ditch. Perhaps the killer, or killers, had been aiming the body into the ditch. Instead it had rolled all the way down the embankment, and came to rest against the wire. Either way, the detectives' thinking was leaning towards two individuals having been involved, due to the difficulty of hoisting that body over the three-foot guard rail.

* * *

Finally something was working in favor of authorities making the connection; appreciating the probability that this murder was not the result of an isolated incident. Lissa Kastin's murder was deemed newsworthy, and reporting in the papers was extensive. She was a "nice girl", well-educated, from a good family, and she was found dead in staunchly middle-class Glendale, the neighborhood whose dull conservatism had inspired *Mildred Pierce* and *The Postman Always Rings Twice*.

When Salerno heard that a young woman had been found naked and strangled in a ravine off Chevy Chase Drive, his ears pricked and he decided to pay an immediate visit to the Glendale PD.

After pooling information with the Glendale detectives, he began to see some clear links to the Miller murder. Like Judy, Lissa had been found nude, and had been strangled by ligature. While Lissa had been found in Glendale, six or seven miles from where Judy had been discovered, in a sprawling city linked by the freeway system, that was actually close. Midway between the two locations was Hollywood, with further connections between the murders revealed in the fact that it appeared both girls had been abducted there.

Lissa's car was eventually found half a block away from her apartment. It was unlocked. The Glendale detectives found a key to the car's hood, but not the ignition, inside Lissa's apartment; and the apartment had been secured. Lissa had last been seen leaving the Healthfaire restaurant about nine the evening before she was found.

It was strange that Lissa's car had been found a ways from her apartment, not in the complex. It looked like she had been abducted from her car before she even made it home.

Why would she pull over before she reached her destination? Possibly because she knew her killer.

The other possibility was that the killer was someone in a position to make her pull over.

Cops, or guys posing as cops.

\* \* \*

After visiting the site, Salerno agreed with the Glendale officers that it would have taken two men to hoist Kastin's lifeless body over the guardrail. The next step was to visit the Coroner's office and compare the bodies of Miller and Kastin. This would help either refute or confirm his suspicions that they were the work of the same perps.

Salerno was the methodical type. He had called prior and asked to have Judy and Lissa placed side by side for the visual examination. He wanted a quick visual read on any links between the MO.

Forensic criminal profiling was a relatively embryonic science in the seventies, and the notion of "serial killer" wasn't even in wide currency. That concept's origins are most often attributed to former FBI agent Robert Ressler, whose coining of the term at the end of the decade was necessitated by a surge of similar killings all over America.

This was in fact the dawn of the age of serial murder. Within a matter of years, you would be able to buy merchandise stamped with the faces of Bundy, Gacy and Ramirez. Salerno had no such inklings of the future as he walked into the coroner's office. Even so, he was an experienced homicide detective and he knew that the marks a killer leaves on a body are a clue to his identity. They are, as distasteful as the analogy is, like an artist's strokes on a canvas. They always leave a trace of their creator behind. The trauma on the body is a kind of language, a symbolic communication. It tells of the killer's drive, his motivation, the essence of what he is about.

With the dead women laid next to each other, Salerno saw that Lissa bore the exact same ligature marks around the neck, wrists and ankles that Salerno had seen on Judy. Not only that, they were in almost identical locations, and angled in a similar way. It was, he later said, literally as if he were looking at a Xerox copy.

His suspicions confirmed, Salerno went over the coroner's other findings. Lissa, like Judy, had been raped, although in this instance there was no evidence of sodomy. Kastin was not a prostitute or a part of the Hollywood street culture. The fact that there had been sexual violation of the body meant that the similar evidence of rape in the examination of Miller (and Yolanda Washington, although the police had not connected the dots there yet) could no longer easily be written off as a side effect of the fact that those women were turning tricks for money.

If all women had been dispatched by the same killer, rape was part of the motivation. What they had on their hands was a sex killer: the type for whom murder provides a sexual thrill that extends and enhances the gratification of the act alone.

# Chapter 6

Suddenly everyone was sitting up and paying attention. Los Angeles law enforcement swung into action. It was now thought that the murder of Judy Miller, a homicide that had earlier aroused little concern, might just be the beginning of a much bigger problem—a problem not just for Hollywood, but for "the people".

And if Lissa Kastin could be abducted at random from the street, between her car and the few steps to her door, then any young woman could be. Los Angelenos would not stand for this. Whoever was behind it had to be stopped, and quickly.

Detectives from the Glendale and Los Angeles jurisdictions met together after being been tipped off by the coroner's office to look for more connections between the Miller and Kastin murders. Their hope was that by pulling their information together something new would come to light, but progress was severely hampered by the lack of physical evidence; bodies that had been stripped and dumped thwarted efforts to link the victims to possible perpetrators or to a murder location.

They were beginning to entertain the possible existence of a serial murderer. They were fairly confident it was two men they were looking for, and it was possible they were cops or guys posing as police officers.

And they were good. They knew what they were doing. They seemed to have a refined plan and method, one that both flouted their skills and enabled them to escape detection.

All in all, the conclusions the cops could draw from the available facts were terrifying. Two men gaining the trust of potential victims by posing as public authorities. Two men who now appeared to attack indiscriminately, posing a threat not only to prostitutes but to average women. Two men who intimately knew the Los Angeles freeway system, who took advantage of its dual power to connect and isolate. Women abducted, killed and dumped in disparate locations across the county, across multiple police jurisdictions.

The cops, for now, remained silent on their private speculations. They were well aware that publicizing connections between the murders or alerting the public to the existence of a hypothetical serial killer might not only create unnecessary hysteria, but could further hinder the investigation. If the killers felt their actions were under the spotlight, they might alter their modus operandi to throw the police off the trail and evade detection. The similarities in the MOs were really the only solid clue the police had, so they decided to reveal as little as possible to the media.

On 10 November, the *Los Angeles Times* ran a small story towards the back of the paper. "TWO GLENDALE SLAYINGS MAY BE LINKED", proclaimed the headline.

There was little information in the article except that the two girls had been strangled in a similar manner, and there was nothing about the possibility of two perpetrators.

Jim Mitchell had been to the body locations for both the Miller and Kastin murders. After speaking with the police he reported only that there had been a murder of a young woman in Glendale similar to the one in La Crescenta.

They didn't quite have a strangler yet, he would later say.

\* \* \*

After Lissa Kastin's body was found, it was apparent to Salerno that whoever had done away with Judy Miller was no casual dabbler in rape and homicide. Compelled by a renewed sense of urgency, he decided to track down Markust Camden again. Salerno was sure that Camden knew more than he was saying. He probably just needed a little nudge to spill the beans.

Salerno only needed to go down to Hollywood and return to Markust's haunt the Fish n' Chips to find his witness.

He bluntly told Camden that he was now a suspect in two murders. They had the body of another young lady over at the city morgue, and they knew she was killed by the same guy that killed Judy Miller. Camden had been the last to see Judy alive, so if he knew anything, now might be the time to speak up.

Markust, usually high-strung, suddenly became paler and sweatier than usual, launching into an impassioned rebuttal.

—I ain't done nothing, swear on my heart! But ... you're right, I didn't tell you the whole story. If I did it would have made me look real bad, and well ... I figured let sleeping dogs lie ...

Salerno probed: well?

—Well the truth is I didn't leave Judy at the Fish n' Chips that night. She come back with me to the Gilbert.

Now Salerno understood. This did indeed make Camden look bad.

—So ... you had sex with her?

Camden nodded.

If Markust had had intercourse with Judy shortly before she died, tests on any semen found inside her body—if it was the same blood type—might place him within a very narrow group of suspects. The guy could be in big trouble.

—Listen, Salerno said, if you're telling the truth, and you got nothing to hide, you'll be in the clear. We just want to find the guy who did this. But make no mistake, this is very serious. You really don't want to be mixed up in this if you can avoid it. Okay?

Camden promised to tell everything.

—Judy was broke. She was hungry. She looked like she hadn't eaten in weeks. I took her down Carney's Railroad Diner for some food. We got hot dogs. After that, she went to turn a trick. A car pulled up alongside her on Sunset. I seen Judy talking to the guy through the diner window, setting up a deal.

—Could you describe this guy? Would you be able to identify him in a photo or a line-up?

—Oh yeah, I got a good look at him. He was dark, you know, could have been ... Puerto Rican. Dark hair, bushy. Big nose. Definitely a big honker. The car was a limo. I'm pretty sure about that. Dark blue limousine.

—And what happened then?

Camden threw his hands up. She got in the car and it took off, he said. It was headed east down Sunset. Turned into a side road, not sure which. That was the last time he saw her.

# Chapter 7

Camden's sighting of the probable suspect was a small, but meaningful win as far as Salerno was concerned.

Little did he—or anyone else—know, a fourth victim already lay decomposing by the side of the Los Feliz off-ramp of the Golden State Freeway.

Twenty-eight-year-old actress and model Jane King was partially hidden by the fallen autumn leaves. She would not be found until 23 November, by which time she had been dead a good two weeks.

On 9 November 1977, Jane ate dinner while watching TV with her roommate, before heading out to her six o'clock acting class at Scientology Manor, now known as Church of Scientology Celebrity Centre International, on Franklin Avenue.

Jane was perhaps typical of the many aspiring actors and actresses who are attracted to Scientology. The Church's clergyman, Jeff Dubron, would later describe her—somewhat creepily given the Church's reputation—as "a young woman trying to find herself". Perhaps Dubron meant that Jane was vulnerable; and she was. Friends described her as shy and self-conscious, an avid dieter and exerciser. Jane was alone in Los Angeles, living with a flatmate she barely knew, looking for success and acceptance in Hollywood. She was also, by any standard, very beautiful, with the willowy figure, long blonde hair, large eyes and precise features which fulfill all the criteria of conventional attractiveness. Modeling gigs had been easy for her to come by, and they helped her pay her way while she waited for the big bucks that come with making it in the entertainment industry.

## A City Owned

After her class finished up, one of Jane's fellow students offered her a lift home. She declined, saying she preferred to take the bus, and left for the bus stop on the corner of Franklin and Tamarind.

When she arrived there she checked the timetable and realized she had just missed one. She would be waiting a good ten to fifteen minutes for the next.

A good-looking young man with dark hair approached, sat down next to her at the shelter, and politely asked when the next bus was due.

Jane didn't usually talk to strangers, but the man seemed very nice, his manner totally low-key and unthreatening. To Jane he even seemed a little naïve and sheltered, like maybe he was new to Los Angeles and didn't know his way around.

Her hunch was right. The man told her he was from Rochester, New York and had only been in Los Angeles a short time. He was still getting to know the city. He joked that he hadn't really taken people seriously when they told him that you needed a car to live in Los Angeles, but now he saw they were right.

Jane commiserated with the friendly stranger about the terrible public transport in Los Angeles, but as far as she was concerned, that was the end of the conversation. She was shy and tended to keep to herself.

But the man kept talking and Jane found herself loosening up, warming to him. He was disarming, so easy to speak with. They shared a run-of-the-mill exchange of small talk, but without the awkwardness she was used to when talking to people she didn't know.

He asked Jane what she did for a living and she told him she was an actress. He now had a perfect opening to drop the nugget that, what with the terrible economy and coming from interstate, he had had no luck so far finding work in his preferred profession of policing or security, but he had been accepted into the sheriff's reserves.

He even showed her his badge—so when the bus was late, and a car came by, driven by an older man her companion at the bus stop identified as his friend "Tony", Jane did something she probably normally wouldn't do, and accepted a ride.

Hypothetically, "Tony" had just randomly been in the area. Jane had no clue that the whole thing was a trap that had been set up well in advance, when the two men had been driving around Hollywood in "Tony's" car, spotted an incredibly attractive young blonde in silver high heels sitting alone at the bus shelter, and decided then and there that she was the one.

Jane told "Tony" that she was just going down to the end of Franklin; she didn't want to put him out or make him go out of his way.

—No problem! Only thing is ... I been out on the road all day. On my way to my last appointment now ... gotta make a quick detour to pick something up at my house. That okay?

The clever man did not want Jane to be alarmed when the car moved off on an unexpected route.

At some point, she probably realized that they had gone well off the planned itinerary, because they left Hollywood altogether and were headed towards Glendale. By that time, she was probably already in manacles.

Jane King had a boyfriend. A few days before she was killed, they had quarreled, and hadn't seen each other since. The boyfriend decided to extend the olive branch on the Wednesday evening, when he called her apartment only to be told by her roommate that she had just left for the acting class that would prove to be her last.

When Jane never returned, her boyfriend and the roommate reported her missing. Her case was handled by the missing persons unit, and they had no cause to connect her fate with that of Judy Miller or Lissa Kastin until her body, bearing the signature five-point ligature marks, was found weeks later near the Golden State.

By then, three further victims would be found.

By then, anytime a young woman disappeared in Los Angeles, the first words that would enter the minds of her loved ones were The Hillside Strangler.

# Chapter 8

Thanksgiving is a hallowed tradition in the United States. It has its origins in English harvest celebrations dating from the Protestant Reformation, which the Puritan founding fathers brought with them to the New World. The Puritan tradition replaced Catholic church holidays with Days of Fasting and Days of Thanksgiving: unexpected disasters and threats to the way of life required fasts; and special blessings and providence, such as a successful harvest, called for festivities called thanksgiving. In 1863, as part of his efforts to foster a sense of American unity between the northern and southern States, Abraham Lincoln proclaimed an annual holiday for Thanksgiving to fall on the final Thursday of November. Intricately bound with their very history and identity, it is as important a holiday for Americans as Christmas is in the rest of the Western world. The November holiday is supposed to be a time of joy and peace, a time for families to come together and appreciate the good things of life.

But Thanksgiving week in Los Angeles, 1977, was memorable for all the wrong reasons. The events of that week were a sadistic joke, a mockery of the holiday's meaning, and nobody who lived in the city through that time would ever forget.

It began innocently enough with a nine-year old boy fossicking in a trash heap near his home. On the afternoon of 20 November, Armando Guerrero and some of his friends took their bikes down to Landa Street, in the Elysian Valley near the Silver Lake Reservoir. This area was familiar to Armando, even though it was not well known to many. Landa Street was quiet, and received little traffic. Armando liked to ride his bike there, and the shady slope below was a secret place where he often found hidden treasures.

Armando and his friends were hunting amongst the junk when his eye caught sight of what appeared to be a couple of store mannequins, laying head to toe. Excited at his discovery, Armando went in for a closer look. He reached for the ankle of one of the mannequins, but quickly recoiled in horror. The ankle had felt squishy, not hard like plastic, and then he saw that a ring of ants was feasting on it.

Armando had never seen a dead body before, but he knew that was what this was. He ran home and told his 17-year-old brother Alonso, who accompanied him back to the trash heap to make sure he wasn't telling tales. Confirming the grim discovery for himself, Alonso telephoned the police.

The policeman who soon arrived on the scene knew that the stiffness which had deceived Armando into thinking he had found two mannequins was rigor mortis. He contacted LAPD Homicide, who sent a team out.

\* \* \*

The spot was dim, well shaded by brush and trees. As Sargeant Dudley Varney made his way there, bending out of the way of the shrubbery, he thought not many folk would even know this place existed. It was just an accident that Armando had uncovered these victims. They might have simply vanished, their fate a mystery forever.

Varney picked his way through discarded moldy mattresses and tossed beer bottles. He knew what he could expect. He knew the victims were two females and that they had been found naked. By now, a lot of people on the force were talking about a spate of stranglings in Los Angeles.

But as they came into view, Varney flinched.

They had been dead a good while, because rot was setting into the bodies. And underneath a hole growing in a moldy cheek, a pair of silver braces glinted.

These were two little girls, barely into their teens.

Varney asked Armando and Alonso if either of them knew the girls. They did not, but Alonso said he'd heard that two girls were missing from St. Ignatius School, in Highland Park. The school had distributed a poster with photographs and descriptions of the girls, and a reward for information. They were Delores Cepeda, twelve, and Sonja Johnson, fourteen.

Varney contacted the school and learned that a priest there had distributed the posters. With the photographs, he was able to make a positive identification. Varney learned that the girls had been missing for a week, and the school had been conducting a massive search of its grounds. Delores and Sonja's parents had also reported the girls missing, and had been frantically searching the neighborhood. It had been their hope that perhaps the girls, who were friends, had simply run off somewhere.

On the very same day, a few short hours before Armando Guerro had been whizzing down Landa Street on his bike, ignorant of the strange turn his day was about to take, Sargeant Varney's partner Detective Bob Grogan was called to the corner of Ramon's Way and Wawona on the other side of the Elysian Valley, between Glendale and Eagle Rock.

The site was nestled in an obscure patch of small suburban streets, surrounded on all sides by houses and lawns; as peaceful and ordinary as could be but for the spectacle of the lifeless naked body of a young woman by the side of a road, only partially shaded by the skimpy arbors of a tree.

The image was jarring in its incongruity. But it also spoke to Grogan of a killer who had gone out of his way. He also must have known the area, even its remotest crannies, very well. Grogan himself had found some difficulty getting to the location, despite his long experience navigating the roads of Los Angeles.

Grogan did not yet know of the forensic details of the Kastin or Miller murders, handled by other jurisdictions.

As the coroner turned the body over, blood oozed out of the girl's rectum. That was the first tell-tale sign of a sexually motivated killer. She had been sodomized, and the evident violence of it was suggestive of a lack of consent. Strangulation marks ringed the girl's neck; further bruising circled the ankles and the wrists.

Grogan leaned forward, focusing his eyes. He blinked. In the crook of the girl's arm there two tiny little red marks nestled in larger pools of green. They were needle marks, the same you would see on any IV drug user.

The victim was otherwise healthy looking, clean and unravaged. A grim intuition flowered in Grogan's mind. He couldn't be sure—later blood tests would confirm his suspicions—but this woman was no junkie.

The puncture wounds were traces of the killer's game, some kind of sick fun he had had with her before finishing her off. She had been tortured.

\* \* \*

Driving back to the unit, Grogan's thoughts were a mishmash. Like Salerno, he was a seasoned homicide cop. Russet-haired and built like a bear, Grogan was known for bluntness and quick temper. Despite his long immersion in Los Angeles and the fact that he had made his home there, he could never quite get around to liking the place. The sunshine, the ocean and the fishing were just fine, but he had seen enough craziness in the last few years to last him a lifetime. He hailed from the northeast, from Boston, and from the kind of simple working-class Catholic communities that were organic to those parts. Los Angeles had always horrified him in its capacity for depravity and its relative lack of proper human values. Even so, he thought he had been there long enough to get used to it. He thought nothing much could shock him anymore. He had just been proven wrong.

Upon their return to the department, Grogan and Varney compared notes and immediately realized the enormity of what had just happened.

They were in no doubt that the three victims had all been killed by the same guy—or guys. The distinctive ligature marks on neck, wrists and ankles was a giveaway. And they were in agreement that there were probably two men behind it. Grogan had seen no drag marks on the body, and no disturbance to the ground around. It was possible that one man had dumped her so effortlessly—a large, strong man. But it was much more likely that two men had hoisted her onto the ground from a car in one swift movement. And since Johnson and Cepeda had been murdered by the same killers, these guys were obviously in the middle of some kind of rampage. The two little girls had been dispatched in a double execution. The decomposed condition of those bodies suggested that they had been killed sometime before the girl found on the other side of the valley, but the difference was a matter of a week, tops.

The woman whose body was found at Ramon's Way was identified as twenty-year old Kristina Weckler, a student at the Pasadena Art Centre of Design who lived alone in an apartment on 809 East Garfield Avenue, in Glendale. Kristina's parents lived in San Francisco, from where Kristina had traveled to study at the design school.

One of Kristina's classmates had reported her missing after she failed to turn up to class. Kristina's friend had gone to her apartment on East Garfield Avenue, and after persuading the building manager to let her in, found it empty. Kristina's car was parked in its usual place in the parking lot.

Kristina was a quiet, conscientious person who preferred to stay in at night and work on her drawings. Knowing her regular habits, all this had set alarm bells ringing, and the friend had immediately called the police.

Grogan learned from Kristina's friend that there had been a party the night before, and Kristina had wanted to attend but had not been invited. There was going to be marijuana at this particular party, and Kristina's friends knew that she did not approve of pot, so she had been left out.

At East Garfield Avenue, Grogan found the home of an orderly, diligent woman with nothing out of place. Her brushes and pencils were arranged neatly at a workstation with a drawing board. The bed had been turned down, as if her tragic misadventure had interrupted preparations for sleep. Several of Kristina's drawings were laid out near her workstation. They were undeniably good: she was a talented young woman.

Staring at them, Grogan was slowly enveloped in a silent, seething rage. She had had hopes and dreams that now stood no chance of fulfillment. This was a fine person, a valuable life, with enormous potential. The killers had used her, obliterated her and thrown her away, as if she were nothing.

There was a notebook on the stand next to the bed. Flipping through, Grogan saw it was a kind of journal, with Kristina's notes about her daily life and small sketches and plans for her drawings.

In amongst the pages Kristina had scribbled an account of a seemingly trivial incident. A resident in the apartment complex named Ken Bianchi had nagged her for a date. He was good looking, but for some reason he gave her the creeps. Kristina politely declined.

She used an interesting analogy to describe the man: he was "like a used car salesman".

The fact that a man had tried coming onto a woman who later turned up murdered, combined with Kristina's characterization of said man, possibly should have raised red flags with Grogan. But the mention of Bianchi had seemed very casual, just one of many notes that Kristina had made in her book. There was nothing to make it stand out, nothing to link it to the murder.

Either Grogan didn't immediately notice the note, or didn't attach any particular importance to it. If he had, he never would have done what he did next.

Grogan was required to turn the notebook in as evidence. However, acting under the influence of emotions grossly disturbed by the circumstances of a case the likes of which he had never seen before, he made a different choice.

Being in Kristina's apartment amongst her things had given Grogan a strange sense of intimacy with the victim. Seeing the condition of Kristina's body—the evidence of her brutal violation, the injection marks suggestive of prolonged torture—had done terrible things to his mind. Heartbreak for Kristina's family prompted him to give the notebook to them, contrary to his duty as a police officer investigating a homicide. Making an unlucky mental gamble, he thought they would get more value from it than the investigators.

Purely by luck, Kristina's father Charles Weckler ultimately returned the notebook to the police.

But, its message and secret was nonetheless destined to be overlooked, for too long.

# Chapter 9

The solving of a crime is a delicate, tenuous thing, so easily derailed by seemingly minor errors and lapses of judgment. It proceeds on the basis of the formation of links between items of information, items which might initially appear unrelated. Unless there is a sudden stroke of luck, a gift from the gods, it is successful only when the slow and tedious process of collecting and analyzing any and all information that arises from a case is followed.

An opportunity had just been missed at East Garfield Avenue. But over at Eagle Rock, Varney's enquiries had just turned up some very useful information. He had located a witness in the abduction of Delores Cepeda and Sonja Johnson.

On the day of their disappearance the girls had been to Eagle Rock Plaza, and had boarded a bus there homeward. A kid on the bus had seen them get off at York Street, not far from their homes. He watched them walk along the street a ways when a sedan slowed besides them. He saw the girls talking to a man through the car window. He was pretty sure there was someone sitting on the passenger side of the vehicle.

When pressed for a description of the car, the boy struggled. Varney decided to "put him under" to loosen up his memory.

Under hypnosis he confidently relayed that the sedan was dark on the bottom and light on the top. Like a police car.

This testimony was important, because it confirmed two points that had thus far only been theories. There were two perpetrators, and they were either police officers, or were posing as cops.

Due to an unfortunate conspiracy of circumstance, Delores and Sonja were perfectly positioned for timid compliance to the demands of any men appearing to be police officers. At Eagle Rock Plaza, right before they were abducted, the two had been shoplifting makeup. Fearful and ashamed of the likely reaction of their parents when it was discovered they had been stealing, they would have done anything the men asked.

The timing of the abduction—now verified by the kid's witness statement—in relation to the state of decomposition of the bodies when they were found, raised the likelihood that the two girls had been in the custody of their killers for some time before they died. Probably a few days.

The overall picture was growing more hideous by the day. Toying with their victims like cats with mice, before putting them out of their misery. Torturing them. Injecting them with poisons.

These killers were sadists without the slightest shred of compassion or humanity. And there seemed to be a sinister progression taking place, a gleeful escalation of ugliness.

Where would it end? Just how bad was this thing going to get?

\* \* \*

The discovery of three bodies in one day prompted the first formal cross-jurisdictional meeting of representatives from the LAPD, Glendale PD and the Sheriff's Department.

All the principal officers who had been involved in the cases so far—Salerno, Grogan and Varney—were present, and by the end, they were sure that Miller, Kastin, Cepeda, Johnson and Weckler had all been murdered by the same killers. Despite the fact that Yolanda Washington had been found without ligature marks on her wrists and ankles, they added her to the list: the MO was otherwise a fit, and the Hollywood connection made it seem even more so.

Shortly after, Daryl F. Gates, then the Los Angeles Chief Inspector of Police, publicly announced the formation of a taskforce under the organizational leadership of the LAPD. Media reporting on the discovery of the two girls and Kristina Weckler on 20 November had been extensive, and now waves of alarm were rising from the public.

The logistical rationale for a taskforce was that a concentration of human resources would permit more rapid interviewing of suspects and would have a greater capacity to tap any public knowledge of the killers in an investigation that was, thus far, sorely lacking in leads.

But the taskforce was also a public relations exercise. The authorities had to appear to be doing something, and quickly. Nobody knew if or when the body of another young woman would turn up on the streets of Los Angeles, but the general feeling was that this was only the beginning.

Lieutenant Sam Bachman of the Los Angeles Sheriff's Office Homicide Unit was given the responsibility of advertising the taskforce's capabilities to the public. His promotional spiel, aired on TV and in the papers, attempted to create the impression of a well-oiled and tech savvy operation.

The team had a visual chart pinned to the wall of the taskforce headquarters in the Parker Center for connecting clues. Bachman helpfully explained that the lines drawn on the chart represented connections in the case. Let's say, he said, that victim one and victim twelve lived in the same apartment block. It would show it right there on the chart!

This chart would eventually wind all the way around the room—evidence both of a great deal of dedication, but also a lack of progress.

The taskforce also had a dedicated computer, the most expensive then available, retailing at an unbelievable fifty thousand dollars. The computer had a cool sci-fi name, reminiscent of Kubrick's *2001*: PATRIC. Patric, like Hal, sounded like a person, but it was supposed to stand for Pattern Recognition and Information Correlation.

The only problem was, PATRIC was more than a slight misnomer for this machine, which actually had no capability to cross-reference clues. Some detectives referred to it, off-record, as a fifty-thousand dollar filing cabinet.

In reality, the taskforce was not much more than a bunch of officers in a room, removed from their usual duties in order to answer phone calls. Those calls soon began arriving in a never-ending stream from a hysterical citizenry whipped to a frenzy by the media, hypervigilant and likely to report the most minor and vaguely suspicious of incidents and encounters.

The authorities had just tripled their workload, and made it harder to distinguish real leads from false ones.

\* \* \*

There was an old rundown bar in downtown Los Angeles, a hangout favored by cops.

Over the years Salerno, Grogan, and Varney had passed each other there many times, without knowing each others' names. In the past they had stuck within their own little groups, within their jurisdictions and units. Now they knew each other, and here they were, united by a common enemy. Interdepartmental rivalries forgotten, it was sheer bliss to just be able to share the burdens of the case and blow off steam.

Over beer and whiskey, they were swapping their thoughts after the announcement of the formation of the taskforce. They were in agreement that it wasn't the great idea it appeared.

—It's a knee jerk reaction, said Grogan; it's politics, window dressing!

—Well, said Salerno drily, it had to be done. It couldn't not be done.

—Yeah, said Grogan, but that's not how cases get solved, is it?

Grogan's whiskey was clearly stoking an indignant fire within. But Salerno was inclined to agree. The work they did required clear, careful thinking. The whole atmosphere from which the taskforce was born ran counter to that. It was an effort to forestall panic. Those efforts had nothing to do with detective work. They were separate functions.

Grogan urged Salerno to stay for another drink, but Salerno wanted to get home. He liked Bob, he liked his passionate style and unvarnished opinions, but he didn't want to join him in getting all upset about the case, and a hangover tomorrow. All of this was taking up too much of his time and his mind already. It didn't seem like it now, but one day, all of this would be over, it would recede in memory, but Frank's wife and children would still be there, needing him. The center may not hold, but the Salernos would.

As Frank drove home on the freeway that night, he thought about Patrick Kearney. This was another guy, recently hauled in, who had been out killing people as if he were casually shooting rabbits. He'd been driving around Cali, picking up young male hitchhikers, filling them with bullets and amusing himself with their dead bodies. Kearney had been killing for years before anyone even realized his victims were missing. There were many sick people in the world; there always had been. But it was the freeway. It was the freeway that was giving these maniacs their day in the sun.

The modern world had much to answer for, concluded Salerno. Speed, convenience, accessibility; all that was great, but there was a downside. In the age of the freeway, people just disappeared; and by the time somebody noticed, another five were dead.

Then, on 23 November, a few days after Kristina Weckler was found, the badly decomposed body of Jane King was discovered by a road worker in brush besides the Los Feliz off-ramp of the Golden State.

# Chapter 10

The *Los Angeles Times* gave the killers the nickname that would stick forever. The media called them the Hillside Strangler, because the bodies of the victims had been dumped on slopes by roadsides and freeways around the city. The nickname also underlined the fact that, so far, the public thought there was only one man behind the murders, even though the police knew there were two.

It was possible that only one man was doing the actual killing, but either way, he had an accomplice who was helping him dispose of the bodies. The coroner's reports also continued to show that, with the exception of Kastin, the victims had had sexual relations with two men before they died. Police, however, kept these facts to themselves. The less information about the case that was aired in the press, the better would be their chances of catching the guys. A suspect who provided facts that tallied with any forensic information couldn't know those facts from media coverage.

News reports stated that the Jane King murder might be linked to a possible further ten that had occurred in recent months. They drew the strongest links between the Thanksgiving killings and the earlier murders of Miller and Kastin, however the taskforce, and the papers, at this time began to widen the net of possible victims, adding more and more names to the list of women who might have been killed by the Hillside Strangler. This troubling pattern would plague the investigation all the way through, adding to public alarm and muddying lines of enquiry.

The expanding victim list certainly evinced the daily reality of homicide in Los Angeles, spiking as the decade approached its end. It also illustrated the predicament of police, who had so little to go on that they began connecting victims merely on the basis of gender and similar modus operandi.

It didn't take much reading between lines of media reports to detect the bewilderment of the investigators. According to the media, King was possibly the eleventh victim in a series of murders of young females whose partially clothed or nude bodies had appeared under bushes and shrubs in the northern suburbs of Los Angeles over the previous month. In fact, none of the Hillside Strangler victims in Los Angeles were found partially clothed; all were found nude.

Commander Phil Booth of the LAPD said city investigators had not ruled out any of the victims as targets of the same killer, but no decision had yet been made to determine that any of the cases were connected either. Striking a gentle tone of defeat, he admitted that because of the dissimilarities in the cases and the ages and backgrounds of the victims, there was a strong chance that a number of the cases weren't connected at all.

Lieutenant Dan Cooke delivered the same message, but with a slightly more menacing overtone, however unintentional. He told the papers they didn't know if the strangler was one man, two men, or a number of men. Pointing to the element of confusion introduced by the city's size, its degree of interconnectedness, and its apparently sizeable population of whackos, he noted that there were similarities in the cases but because they were spread out, it might not have been "one man but two, three, or four doing it."

This was certainly a rosy picture. Two, three, possibly four—or who knows how many—murderers, violating and garroting young women in apparently random attacks all over the city.

The issue was that many women were turning up strangled in Los Angeles, and not all of them were killed by the Hillside Strangler. Some were killed by husbands and former partners, the "mundane" casualties of domestic violence. Others met their ends at the hands of thrill killers, like the Hillside Stranglers—but not the same guys.

Actually, there were several serial killers targeting women in LA in the late seventies. The pool of their victims bled and blurred into one another, making everything just that bit harder to figure out.

One murder the press reported as connected to the case was that of eighteen-year old Jill Barcomb. A runaway from New York living in Hollywood, she was last seen near the corner of Sunset Boulevard and Poinsetta. On 10 November, her nude body was found on a service road off Mullholland Drive, near the home of actor Marlon Brando.

Barcomb had been sexually assaulted and strangled, but there were other departures from the strangler's usual MO. Her skull had been crushed, likely with a bloodied rock that was found nearby at the scene.

The theory that Barcomb was a victim of the Hillside Strangler was encouraged by reports that she was an associate of Judy Miller. Her murder was eventually determined to be the work of Rodney Alcala, the "Dating Game Killer", so named because he appeared on the television show *The Dating Game* as a contestant in the late seventies. At that time, Alcala was already a convicted rapist, and had been chosen as a contestant on the show in spite of this; he had also already killed several women, but this obviously was not known to police at the time. Alcala was convicted on one charge of murder and kidnapping in 1978, but his conviction was overturned. His killing career continued, as did his scrapes with the law, until he was finally caught and sentenced to death in California in 2010 for five murders committed there between 1977 and 1979. He won a date on *The Dating Game* with contestant Cheryl Bradshaw, who refused to go out with him, citing her opinion that he was "creepy". Alcala, allegedly of genius level IQ, was a professional photographer who graduated from UCLA School of Fine Arts. The process of identifying his victims, still underway today, proceeded largely from examination of his collection of photographs; many of his victims had modeled for him.

Another young woman linked in news reports with the Hillside Strangler was Kathleen Robinson, a seventeen-year old student at Hollywood High School who was known to hitchhike around Los Angeles. Her strangled body was found in a parking lot on Pico Boulevard, Wiltshire, on 17 November. In this case there was no evidence of sexual assault, but her name was nonetheless added to the Hillside Strangler victim list.

Even though they didn't even know if Robinson was actually killed by the same men, the taskforce thought they had already broken the case open when a call came through from a guy called George Shamshack, who claimed to be the man who strangled Kathleen and dumped her in the parking lot in Wiltshire.

When the officer asked for more details, it should have been apparent that Shamshack knew only the sketchiest information about the murder from press reports.

Shamshack's background should have also raised suspicions about the authenticity of his confession: he was an escaped prison inmate from Massachusetts with no ties to Los Angeles. But this didn't stop the police from arresting Shamshack merely on the basis of this confession—and another guy who he named as his accomplice: one Peter Jones, a Beverly Hills handyman. They then strategically informed the press that a suspect had been detained in the Hillside Strangler case.

It turned out that Shamshack was wanted dead by a number of other inmates up in Massachusetts, and was hoping to get himself jailed or at least buy himself some time in Los Angeles so he wouldn't have to go back there.

As for Peter Jones, the only reason Shamshack had named him was because he was the only person he vaguely knew in Los Angeles. The handyman was completely bewildered when he was arrested and had no useful information to give police about the case, despite being the most helpful and cooperative kind of suspect. He was immediately freed, but the entire farce severely damaged his reputation in Los Angeles: he lost his job, received death threats, and had his apartment window shattered in a drive by shooting. He moved to Maine to start fresh, and eventually won a libel suit against a Boston television station that had named him as a suspect in the case.

The fear that rippled through the community when they read the newspapers and saw the reports on television, fear for wives and daughters, was spreading and mutating like a virus, and had become fear of reputational risk and public retribution in the offices of law enforcement and politics.

Panic makes people irrational. Panic makes people hasty and sloppy. The outcomes are rarely desirable. Behind the efforts at impression management, efforts to reassure everyone the authorities were controlling an uncontrollable situation, was a genuine sense of powerlessness.

Panic was about to tear Los Angeles apart.

# Chapter 11

Lauren Wagner seemed like the girl next door. At eighteen she was still living with her parents and siblings in an unpretentious rambler on Lemona Street, near Sepulveda Boulevard in the San Fernando Valley.

Lauren remained at home while she completed her studies at a nearby business college, where she was studying to become a legal secretary, but she liked to be independent. She worked part-time at a dime store, and she didn't like to accept cash or favors from her parents—Joe Wagner would sometimes go and fill the gas tank of her car on the sly, when she wasn't at home. She contributed to the house on an equal footing with the adults, cooking thanksgiving dinner for the whole family and making dresses for her sisters.

Joe and Judy Wagner didn't know everything about their daughter, however. Like the fact that the boyfriend she had been seeing lately was a married man. There was another side to Lauren, and as she got ready for an assignation with her lover on the evening of 28 November, it was this other side that was in charge.

Lauren was excited about the date, and took extra care with her clothes and make-up. When she walked down the stairs to head out the door, Judy was in the kitchen. She quietly gasped at how lovely her daughter looked. Lauren was an attractive girl: slender, with fair unblemished skin and long auburn red hair. When she went to special effort, she looked sensational.

Lately, everyone had been talking about the Hillside Strangler. Everyone was scared for their daughters, nobody wanted their girls going out alone at night. Judy felt a pang of faint misgiving, a gentle wave of anxiety as she stood in the kitchen with her daughter before she left. She brushed it away. Lauren was an adult now. She was smart and sensible. She knew all about the strangler, and she promised to be home by ten. She always did exactly what she said she was going to do, so there was no reason to doubt her. But she looked so bright and trusting and vulnerable standing there in her pretty outfit. Judy lightly touched Lauren's cheek, and told her to be careful.

Lauren went to meet her boyfriend, and the two made love for several hours. She left him and drove home to Lemona Street at around 9:30 pm. She was on a high as she approached her house, and the last thing on her mind was the Hillside Strangler. And what did she have to fear the strangler for when she was just a few doors from her house?

But as soon as Lauren slowed, there they were. They pulled up beside her. Lauren mightn't have thought anything was amiss—just some guys in a vehicle—or she might have been trying to make a bolt for it. Either way, she attempted to get out of her car.

Across the street, Cesar, a Doberman belonging to the Wagner's neighbor Beulah Stofer, started barking loudly.

Mrs. Stofer, sickly and middle-aged, shuffled out to the front of her house to find out what all the drama was about.

She knew something bad was going on, but she froze. She stood transfixed on the lawn behind the bushes, and watched as Lauren was dragged by two men into a car, a sedan, dark-colored on the bottom and white on top. One of the men was tall, with black hair and fair skin, pockmarked around the neck. The other was shorter, older, with a wild curly mane.

Lauren screamed as the men shoved her into their car: *You won't get away with this!*

Then, just like that, the door slammed shut, and the car sped away.

Beulah covered her mouth with her hand and swallowed hard. She knew what she had just seen.

As she walked back into the house, wondering what she should do, who she should call, Lauren's words rang in her ears. It seemed like she knew who the men were, and as they drove her into the night, she must have known already what her fate would be. How terrifying. How utterly, utterly terrifying.

Beulah didn't have to ponder her next move for long. That particular conundrum was solved for her. It wasn't much later that the telephone rang. Even though it was late, Beulah hesitantly picked up the receiver. A male voice with an east coast accent spoke:

—You the lady with the dog? You better keep your trap shut about what you seen. You say anything to anyone, you're as good as dead.

Beulah, scared out of her wits, decided to do just as the man said.

* * *

The following morning, upon waking the Wagners went to check on Lauren and realized she had never come home the night before. They had gone to bed before ten, when Lauren was due back from her date.

Now, grasping that Lauren had been missing a whole night, Joe Wagner told himself that she had got caught up with her boyfriend, and hadn't called to let them know because it was so late.

That wasn't like her though, and it wasn't long before Joe knew for certain that any such comforting rationalization held no water. Looking outside, he saw Lauren's yellow Mustang parked across the road. He went out to the street to investigate further, and saw that the driver side door had been left ajar, and the pilot light was still on. This was bad. This was very bad.

Joe immediately went door-knocking to find out if neighbors had seen or heard anything. When he spoke to Beulah Stofer she was reticent, but eventually admitted that she had heard Lauren arguing in the street with a man or maybe two men. Then she had heard a car speed off. Lauren's Mustang had been parked in the street since about ten the night before.

—My God! Joe said. Why didn't you come knock?

Beulah told him she hadn't actually been sure it was Lauren. She thought it might have been just some girl arguing with her boyfriend.

Her explanation trailed off at the end; Joe was less than convinced. Something was off about it. It was as if Beulah knew more than she was saying. But he didn't have time to worry about that now. If there was any chance Lauren was alive somewhere, he had to act. He immediately went home, called the police, and reported Lauren missing.

The Hillside Strangler had been in the back of Joe's mind as soon as he discovered Lauren had never come home. He might have been wrong, and he really hoped he was, but he let himself be guided by the grim foreboding that was building with each passing moment and every new piece of information that came to light. So far everything was pointing in the one ghastly direction.

So when the officer who took his call told him that it was too early to report Lauren missing, and that a full twenty-four hours had to elapse before they could do anything, he thought on his feet and decided to report the story Beulah had told him as if he had witnessed it himself. He said he'd seen Lauren pulled into a car by two men. They had taken her away before he could do anything to stop it.

It wasn't a lie so much as a minor variation on the truth. In any case it worked. The cops came out to Lemona Street immediately.

Joe didn't have to wait long for confirmation of his worst fears. That morning Detective Bob Grogan was called out to 1217 Cliff Drive, in the hills between Glendale and Mount Washington. Lauren's naked strangled body had been found by the side of the road, her torso partly concealed by brush, but her legs sticking right out onto the pavement.

Any person passing by in a car on their way to work that morning would have clearly seen the body, which was how it had come to the attention of police so quickly.

The same, now tiresomely familiar, pattern of bruising around the wrists, ankles and neck told Grogan that this young woman had met her fate at the hands of the same killers who had murdered Kristina Weckler.

This time, however, there was a slightly new calling card.

In Kristina's murder, Grogan had seen evidence of torture in the puncture wounds on her arms. This victim bore some unusual lesions on her hands. Looking closer, Grogan felt sure they were burn marks, however he couldn't tell exactly how they had been made. There was also a sticky substance on the woman's hands, likely adhesive residue from a tape such as duct or gaffer tape. There was nothing else on the woman's body, but a sticky substance on her breasts: possibly semen or saliva.

These pieces of evidence would be lab tested for further clues that would hopefully point the way to the murderers. What was clear at this point was that the men responsible were experimenting with their methods; so deeply involved were they in their secret world of killing that they relished in inventiveness, getting a kick out of ever darker and more elaborate means of dispatching their prey.

Grogan now had the unenviable task of speaking with Judy and Joe Wagner. How was he supposed to explain to a shattered mother or father just what had happened to their daughter? In the end, there were no words. He just had to try to do his best: be truthful and only give the necessary minimum of horrendous detail.

It was one of the hardest parts of the job. Only a short time had passed since he had met with Charles Weckler, the father of Kristina Weckler. One of the nicest, most polite men he had ever met, and he had dealt with it all with such good grace, even though you could see underneath the effort his heart breaking to a million pieces. Nothing could prepare you for those conversations. Now he had to do it all over again.

\* \* \*

The property at Lemona Street was already swarming with reporters when Grogan arrived. The jostling, greedy mass, wielding notebooks and microphones, confirmed that with Lauren's murder—the third in a span of days—the game had turned some unfathomable, deadly corner. Los Angeles was in uncharted territory.

Grogan himself felt like he had aged a decade in the past week. As he approached the house, Joe Wagner was on the porch fending off a series of questions.

—Mr. Wagner, said a reporter, why do you think your daughter was abducted?

—I don't know, he said. Because she was a girl?

As he and Grogan moved inside the house, he immediately fessed up that he hadn't actually seen "it".

It was Mrs. Stofer, he explained. A couple doors down. She told him she heard Lauren talking to some men in the street, and they took her away in a car. But Joe had to do something to get the cops down. They said he had to wait twenty-four hours; that was just too long. He knew something terrible had happened to Lauren. He knew it was the strangler.

—I just wish I hadn't been asleep, Joe said, fighting back tears; I was asleep in my bed while they took my daughter away and killed her.

The Wagners were a nice, ordinary family, living in a respectable suburban house, just quietly trying to get along in crazy times. Observing their interaction, it quickly became apparent to Grogan that they were exceptionally tight knit, and the loss of Lauren, and the circumstances around it, would devastate the family—permanently.

Grogan completely empathized with Joe's little fib to the officers, but it did put a different slant on the investigative work that needed to be done during this visit. It was Mrs. Stofer he really needed to talk to. Joe said that Beulah had never reported what she had seen or heard, and that he had had to go knocking on her door to find out what happened to Lauren.

This wasn't exactly a ringing endorsement of her as a witness; but once he spoke to Mrs. Stofer, Grogan realized there was a very reasonable explanation for why she hadn't spoken up earlier. She was scared out of her mind.

After some prodding, and in between asthmatic wheezes, Beulah told Grogan about the frightening mystery phone call she had received the night of the murder. She was scared that if she told anyone what she knew, the strangler was going to come after her.

Grogan reassured her that the police would protect her. She was the only eyewitness in the case so far who had possibly seen both of the men, and he needed her to tell him everything.

Cesar was barking, Beulah said. She went to the front of the house and looked out the window, and she saw Lauren struggling with two men. She came across firm and convincing with her physical description of the men. She was absolutely sure that one was older and shorter than the other one. He had curly hair. The younger, taller man had acne scars on his neck. Yes, she would be able to identify them from a photo or line-up. She had seen the men clearly.

But something wasn't adding up for Grogan. How had she been able to observe that the younger man had acne scars on his neck from behind the windows? Mrs. Stofer had poor eyesight, and it had been dark out.

Grogan believed Mrs. Stofer's account, but he had a feeling she had changed aspects of her story, possibly out of shame that she had not reported the incident earlier. He thought she had probably gone outside and observed the killers from the front yard, possibly behind the front fence or the hedge. They had seen her as clearly as she had seen them: otherwise, why would she have received the threatening phone call?

By saying she had witnessed the incident from inside the house, Mrs. Stofer could maintain the appearance that she wasn't exactly sure what she had seen, and therefore had not reported it.

Grogan decided there was more to the story than Beulah told him, but he probably wasn't going to get it out of her straight away. She was still very frightened, and clearly the interview had exhausted her. He would go back to talk to her again later.

# Chapter 12

The circumstances around Lauren Wagner's abduction and murder possibly offered another missed opportunity to close in on the perps, and it isn't precisely clear if it was ever followed up, and if not, why not.

Presumably whoever made the threatening phone call to Mrs. Stofer was one of the men, or someone connected with them. It wasn't possible for an individual to obtain a telephone number for a subscriber merely by providing a street address, without a subscriber name, unless that person had a personal contact inside the telephone exchange willing to do a favor. Thorough questioning of the staff at the exchange might well have revealed the identity of the mystery caller with an east coast accent.

As it was, the killers were still out there, and on 30 November, reporting on the murder of Lauren Wagner was all over the papers in Los Angeles—the headline story for every major publication.

It was ten days since the bodies of Johnson, Cepeda and Weckler had been found; a week since Jane King was discovered moldering next to the freeway; a day since Lauren Wagner's cold body turned up on the pavement of a suburban street in north Los Angeles.

Five bodies in just over a week.

Whoever the strangler was, he was no doubt enjoying his new global notoriety; everyone knew who he was now—everyone, that is, except the cops, to whom he seemed to remain stubbornly invisible.

Joe Wagner's conversation with the reporter was widely circulated.

Why was Lauren killed? *Because*, Joe had said, *she was a girl.*

The frustrated reply of a devastated man to a dumb, insensitive question. For his part, Joe was bewildered at a subtle insinuation he detected in the reporter's words: that Lauren had somehow done something to bring her own rape and murder upon herself, as outrageous as that was.

On the other hand, perhaps the question was meant to shore up comforting delusions of control in the face of this insidious threat. The early victims had been targeted because they were doing something wrong, living the wrong lifestyle. As for Lauren, well, maybe she shouldn't have been out late at night, dressed in those clothes.

Joe Wagner shut that reporter down fast. Lauren's only crime was to be a girl. It was the right answer. The only answer that anybody could come up with.

And within that answer lay the fear. These men weren't just killing whores or street kids; the only criteria they held for their targets was that they be young women or girls. Beyond that, anything went; they could be rich or poor, black or white, suburban schoolgirls or prostitutes.

Who the women were, the individual details of their lives, whatever they had done or not done, did not matter to the killers in the least. It was a crusade; they had been abused and desecrated, then snuffed out, in the most personal way—and yet, it was nothing personal.

The abductions and dumpings were occurring in a wide area, which appeared to be centered on Hollywood and Glendale, but spread almost as far as the county borders to the northeast. And victims were being snatched off streets and dragged into cars literally as they travelled from their vehicles to their front doors. All of that meant no woman was safe anywhere.

The statement provided by Beulah Stofer confirmed the detective's suspicions they were hunting not one man, but two, and that they were using a police ruse to lure the girls.

She, like the boy on the bus, had described a car with a dark bottom and a white top. A car with a black body and white roof was the standard color scheme of LAPD cruisers. It also appeared that, at least initially, the victims had gone willingly with their attackers. Cepeda and Johnson's parents had said, with a note of unintentional irony, that they had taught their girls to avoid strangers, but that police officers were safe and trustworthy.

And then there was the cleanness of the bodies, the absence of defensive wounds. Yes, the women had been bound, but prior to that, it appeared that they had not felt they were in danger.

The police were now quite certain that the men they were looking for were posing as cops—or, even more troubling—were legitimately officers themselves, operating well outside the law.

The authorities were beyond reluctant to share these suspicions with the public, anxious of fanning the flames of hysteria. But now, they saw that they had little choice. It was either that, or be held responsible the next time a woman was found murdered in the streets. They had to give women the chance to defend themselves.

The taskforce issued a media release warning women driving alone to beware being stopped in dark, isolated areas by automobiles that appeared to be police vehicles. They reminded them that they may keep their doors locked and demand an officer's credentials. Of course, if the killers were themselves cops, that final piece of advice was going to be of little help.

Los Angelenos wondered when and where the next body would turn up. Would it be someone they knew? A friend? A friend's daughter? Your own daughter? Was the killing going to stop, or—unimaginable—was it going to get worse? With it now being known that the murderers were likely posing as police, or could be cops themselves, the question on women's lips everywhere was: "Who can you trust?"

And then, as Salerno would later say, all hell broke loose.

"The Southlands New Neighbor: Fear" proclaimed the headline of an article in the *Los Angeles Times* on 3 December 1977.

Women, it said, were only leaving their homes and workplaces during daylight hours, and only in company. Two nurses at Glendale Memorial Hospital, Patricia Bazzell and Janice Ritchie, told the reporter they always went out together to do their shopping early, because they didn't want to be alone—even in the day.

The communities around Glendale, Highland Park and Eagle Rock caught the fear virus when the press frenzy began at the end of Thanksgiving week, when the stripped and violated bodies of nice white middle class girls started appearing on their tidy suburban streets. The effect was obvious and immediate. At night an eerie quiet descended. If women were out, they were in the company of men. But mostly, it was only men on the streets.

And how could it be otherwise? The bodies were a message, a warning to all women.

## A City Owned

Retreat, they said; go back into your homes. The city does not belong to you. Something terrible is coming your way.

\* \* \*

Shopkeepers, especially at Eagle Rock Plaza, complained about the downturn in business. But some retailers were doing much better than they had before the murders.

Guns and ammunition had always been popular in Los Angeles. But now, they were flying off the shelves. Sporting goods stores reported that sales of baseball bats were surging. More rudimentary weaponry could be had for less money. Many women began stashing lead pipes under the front seats of their cars. Martial arts and self-defense classes were enjoying a boon, and guard dogs weren't just for protecting the home any more.

And then there were the blood chilling moments of paranoia, because nobody knew who he was, what he looked like, where he might be lurking. A young woman told the papers she was visiting friends in Anaheim—far from Glendale—and stopped in a neighborhood store. She suddenly became aware of a man's eyes lingering on her, and freaked, hightailing it out of there. She realized later that subconsciously, she was wondering if he was the killer.

The Hillside Strangler's presence was felt, and feared, everywhere, blurring into the face of any vaguely predatory stranger. While there was hope he would soon be scooped up and thrown behind bars, women had to deal with the daily reality. There was an ill wind in Los Angeles, a scent of doom on the air, born of fear that the killing spree was going to continue, even escalate, and there wasn't a damn thing anybody could do about it. It was certainly hard to rely on the cops to protect them when there was a chance the murderers were cops themselves.

On the streets of Hollywood, confidence in the police was at an all-time low. The women there knew that some of the early victims had been runaways or prostitutes, and some of them had known those victims personally. They were dismissive of police efforts to protect them.

A prostitute named Cheryl told reporters that the police resented them.

—They resent anything to do with a woman selling her body or getting money any way she can. It's up to us to take care of each other.

Women soliciting on the Boulevard and the Strip began to do so only in the company of a friend, with one woman making the deal with the john, and the other taking down his license plate number and a description. They also made a note of any clients that behaved suspiciously or made particularly bizarre or kinky requests, warned other women, and if they could get a cop to listen, filed a report.

Tips from the prostitute community were just a proportion of calls now flooding the lines at the Parker Center. Many of these calls described a familiar, recurring scenario.

*These guys pulled me over and lectured me for something I never done. I thought they were cops but then I realized it wasn't a real cop car.*

*He showed me his badge, but now that I think about it, I don't think it was the real thing.*

*They were acting all tough and mighty, like cops, but I don't think they were cops.*

The women repeatedly reported being harassed for minor and imaginary offences. There was usually something odd either about the vehicles, the officer's uniforms or their badges and equipment—something that was not what you would expect to see with a bona fide operation.

The officers manning the lines, receiving these complaints, grew increasingly troubled. They were aware that there were some guys in Los Angeles that would buy old stripped out highway patrol cars at auctions and fit them out for their own purposes. There were some men who maybe liked to play dress ups and have a laugh. But it now appeared to them that this phenomenon was more widespread than initially thought. It was bizarre. It was as if there was a shadow society out there mimicking them, improperly messing in their business. Because certainly not all of these calls could have been describing encounters with the stranglers.

The calls also worried the taskforce, because yet another confusing element was being thrown into their investigation. Not only did they not know if there was more than one man or team responsible for the killings, they now had to contend with a raft of potential suspects who looked and acted in the same ways that the real perps did.

All officers involved in the investigation were now put on notice to keep an eye out for vehicles that looked like patrol cars and where possible, check them out, as well as their drivers.

On the other hand, the taskforce could not dismiss the unpleasant possibility that the Hillside Stranglers had emerged from within their own ranks.

While they always hoped it was an exceptional occurrence, a bad hire slipping through their screening and recruitment procedures was far from unheard of; and some men were attracted to the study of police procedure for the very reason that such knowledge could help them to better carry out and conceal crime. So while they continued hunting the killers in the community, they now also had to begin the irksome process of an internal investigation of their own people.

They started by looking at beat officers who were working in areas where abductions and dumpings had occurred. Logbooks were examined to ascertain the location of each officer on the nights of the murders, and to verify the activities of that officer at the time in question.

If a cop was in the area but not on a specific call, or elsewhere without an alibi, further investigation including surveillance might be ordered. This process led to the questioning of some officers, but eventually, all of them were cleared. That in itself was a relief to the investigators; but they were still no closer to finding their men.

LA cops were by no means above reproach in their dealings with the city's women, which complicated everything even further.

One day a call came through to the LAPD from a young woman who thought she'd just had a brush with the stranglers. She was driving when what appeared to be two vice officers pulled her over. They had a red light but were driving an unmarked vehicle. When one of the cops spoke to her through her window she was intimidated by what she perceived as a leery manner, and deciding that these guys might be the killers, had screeched off through the intersection. They had showed her a badge, the number of which she had remembered and included in her report later. The cops had pursued her for a while before she lost them.

When the department investigated, they learned that the two men in the unmarked car were in fact vice officers. They had gotten turned on after watching prostitutes all night and decided to make what they referred to as a "pussy stop" at the conclusion of their shift—in other words, they were trying to pick the woman up for sex. This was a common enough practice amongst cops, but in the context of the investigation—or in any context really—it was utterly embarrassing.

The wider angle to this incident was the existence of a dubious male culture within the rank and file of Los Angeles police, not to mention the long history of inappropriate police involvement in prostitution activities. It was not above certain cops to avail themselves of the very services they were supposed to be shutting down. Some officers had even been known to extract sexual favors from women as the price for letting them off a charge. Sexual exploitation and brutality against prostitutes had always gone hand in hand with policing them. There were rapes, beatings and harassment by the cops.

The irony, then, was that some less noble elements of the force held attitudes to prostitutes not too far removed from those of the perps they were supposed to be going after.

* * *

—It's a circus, Frank, Grogan said one night at the bar.

They had just heard the news that the size of the taskforce was being increased to nearly a hundred officers. They were needed to take all the calls that had nothing to do with the case.

The authorities squirmed in the face of the public's rising fear and recriminations. Gates had been on the news trying to put a good face on things, conveying the impression that they were systematically working through their leads, and closing in on their targets. Nothing could have been further from the truth. There were no murder scenes, barely any physical evidence, and no viable suspects. Then, the taskforce made the brilliant move of posting a $140,000 reward for information leading to capture, and every Tom, Dick and Harry was calling in, saying his neighbor or his boss or whoever was on his shitlist that week was "the guy".

—Yeah, said Salerno; but you gotta think how this all plays out in the bigger picture. Up top. If we don't find these guys, they lose office. But then that's good for the other side, isn't it?

Mayor Tom Bradley's conservative opponents were making him look weak on violent crime. If they were in office, they said, this would never be happening. The killer would already be in the can.

—Politics, Grogan sneered.

—It's funny, said Salerno, people expect us to find these guys as of yesterday, but it isn't the way it used to be. Maybe I'm wrong but I feel like people used to kill each other for legitimate reasons. Now it's just entertainment.

—And the world is just getting so complex, said Grogan. I mean look at that taskforce. There's no … control anymore. But they keep telling everyone that there is.

Salerno and Grogan missed the days when they could do their jobs unencumbered by excessive bureaucracy and media hoopla. They had so little confidence in the investigation that they were keeping some of their own information, including the identity of their key witnesses, from the taskforce. They didn't trust it would not get leaked to the press, possibly endangering more lives.

In the early weeks of December 1977, about the only positive for investigators was that what they had dreaded most—an escalation of the pattern set by the murderers in late November, and a spiraling of the body count—did not materialize. The first two weeks of the month were quiet, and no more young women appeared dead on suburban streets and hillsides.

Salerno and Grogan began to hope that the killers had been driven underground by the intensifying investigation. Perhaps they had been picked up on an unrelated charge, or they had moved onto new hunting grounds, or even better, were themselves dead. But they were wrong.

The Hillside Stranglers had merely taken a brief hiatus, gathering their energies for a brutal shock about to be unleashed on the city.

# PART TWO
# A CITY OWNED

# Chapter 13

Seventeen-year-old Kimberly Diane Martin might have been young, but she was already a tough and experienced practitioner of her trade. Like all the girls in Hollywood she knew about the Hillside Strangler, and wishing to avoid the dangers of street soliciting, had signed up to work with an outcall agency that would screen clients.

The agency operated under the cover of a nude modeling service, although its trading name, Climax, left little doubt as to the true nature of its operations. On the evening of 13 December, a call came through to the agency from a man identifying himself as Mike Ryan. Mr. Ryan said the wife was out of town for the first time in a couple years. He wanted them to send out a model; someone blonde, preferably with black underwear.

The agency receptionist told Mr. Ryan she would find a girl matching his request and have her call him back. But when she took his number, her suspicions were aroused. It was the kind of number that usually identified a payphone, not a private residence. She had been trained to be on the lookout for such calls, as they were typically pranks. She tried to smoke the client out.

—Sir, is that a payphone you're calling from?

—Hah, you know it's funny. A lot of people seem to think this is a payphone. It must be a digit in the number or something.

—That must be it. The reason I thought it was a payphone is because the fourth digit of the number is a "9". It's a payphone.

The receptionist's response had tried to strike the balance between politeness and calling the potential client out, but Mr. Ryan ignored any such subtleties, barreling right over her concerns with a ready explanation.

—That must be it, or the fact that you hear my TV in the background. Would you like me to turn it off?

The "TV" noise the caller referred to was in fact the sound of patrons milling and talking in the lobby of the Hollywood public library, where the man was indeed calling from a public payphone.

The receptionist called the operator to verify the number, but in a cruel twist, the operator gave the response that usually indicated the number was attached to a private residence. "Sorry ma'am, we can't give out that information." The fate of Kimberly Martin, an attractive young blonde that night on shift with Climax, was effectively sealed.

"Mike Ryan" had given his address as apartment 114, 1950 Tamarind Avenue, Hollywood, where Kimberly—who traded under the name Donna—was sent sometime between nine and ten.

Kimberly drove over to Tamarind in her Oldsmobile and parked on the street a little ways down from the complex. She wore, as requested, black underwear, black stockings, and a black dress. Around her neck Kimberly also had a more personal item: a gold necklace with a ram's horn shaped pendant.

The Tamarind Apartments were relatively new, built in the sixties, but already somewhat worn-looking due to high tenancy turnover. It was a transitional neighborhood with a lot of renters. Apartment 114 was on the ground floor.

Kimberly knocked and a young man with dark hair and a mustache opened the door. When she walked in, she immediately knew something weird was going on.

The apartment was new and clean, with white-painted walls and ruby-red carpet. Too new. Too clean. There were no furnishings. The apartment was completely bare.

\* \* \*

Up on the fourth floor, Sari Knapheis, a widow who lived alone, was getting ready for bed. She heard several screams, scuffling, commotion. She heard the sounds of footsteps, people running up and down the hallways.

She wasn't about to open her door and find out what was going on. She heard screaming and hollering every night, and nothing good was ever going to come of poking your nose into the business of the kind of people who lived in that building.

Another resident at the complex, who lived on the first floor, heard a woman very clearly scream out: *someone's trying to kill me!*

It wasn't the kind of scream he would usually associate with a domestic dispute. It was, he later said, the worst scream he had ever heard.

A little before midnight, while Kimberly was being raped and tortured, Lois Lee, the prostitution researcher, was getting ready for bed when her telephone rang.

The call was from the Climax Agency, where a number of girls Lee was well acquainted with through her research and advocacy work were on the books. One of those women was Kimberly Martin, who was now officially AWOL; she had never come back from her last appointment, they told her.

It was possible there was a more innocent explanation for Kimberley's disappearance, but with the stranglers loose on the streets, and it now being known they looked like cops, Lee worried much more about the women than usual.

Lois took down the phone number and address Mike Ryan had given the Climax receptionist. After some digging around, she was able to trace the number to the Hollywood public library.

In the best-case scenario this had been a prank call and Kimberly had been sent to a non-existent job, and there was some other explanation for why she had failed to check back in with the agency. But nothing Lois had discovered so far was allaying her worries. She decided to get into her car and go straight over to Tamarind.

Lee saw Kimberly's car parked in the street, but at apartment 114, nobody answered the door, and from outside, through the glass patio doors, she could see that the place was unfurnished and unoccupied.

With a sickening certainty forming inside, Lois next called the sheriff's department. The responding officer told her that a missing person report could not be lodged until 24 hours had elapsed, and that since Kimberly was a prostitute, and prostitutes were renowned flakes, it wouldn't be high on their list of priorities anyway.

Undeterred, Lee went into the Sheriff's office in person to demand they follow up on Kimberly. She was left waiting for two hours before she was questioned by officers.

By that time, Kimberly was dead.

The call came through early on 14 December, when the sky had just begun to fade. Two paperboys found her while on their regular morning route along Alvarado Street in Echo Park.

Salerno arrived to a scene already swarming with reporters and curious, gawking residents. Cars jammed the road and getting to the site was like navigating an obstacle course.

Alvarado Street is one of the longest in Los Angeles, and at its southern end, a major traffic thoroughfare linking the north and south of the city. The northern end of the street however is primarily residential. Snaking atop hills overlooking the city centre, it is highly sought after by property hunters for its sweeping views of Los Angeles' night lights.

Salerno crossed the curb at the empty lot at 2006 North Alvarado and looked down.

The empty lot fell away from the street down the hillside. There was Kimberly, splayed naked on her back on the steep grassy hill, a few feet from the road, her spread-eagled body facing all the traffic, buildings and pedestrians of downtown Los Angeles. She had been placed obscenely, her vulva pointing almost directly at City Hall off in the distance. In fact, the body would have been clearly visible from inside that building.

Well, thought Salerno, isn't that just a big fuck you.

Such an unspeakably brazen dumping could only be some kind of statement; a demonstration of superiority, a smug rebuke to the authorities who had so evidently failed to halt their rampage.

The detectives had already observed that the killers were ramping up their excitement and pleasure by varying their methods: Kristina Weckler had been injected with a cleaning fluid, and the lesions on Lauren Wagner's hands suggested the men had indulged in some creative method of burning torture, perhaps electrocution. Now it appeared they were playing to the media, delighting in their growing celebrity, taunting the city with their skills in evading capture.

The murder of Kimberly Martin was terrorism. We own Los Angeles, it declared. We own this city; and we own you.

\* \* \*

If it was notoriety the murderers were seeking, they finally got it in spades. The *Los Angeles Times* ran news of the murder as their cover story on 14 December, along with a horrendously provocative aerial shot of Kimberly's body splayed on the vacant lot at Alvarado, and the headline in large block black letters, "Strangler Strikes Again".

Following its publication, fear and outrage spilled over again. TV news segments repetitively banged on two themes: the cop's lack of progress, and the terror of the community.

A reporter did a vox pop piece in and around Glendale. One young woman's view of the Hillside Strangler was heavily featured all the over the evening news.

—He's sick. Just ... sick, she said, shaking her head from side to side.

\* \* \*

The pressure was never greater to crack the case and get this freak off the streets.

How the detectives handled the next phase of the investigation was critical, particularly as they now had—for the first time—promising leads to follow: a physical location, several new witnesses at the apartment complex, and now, a physical description of the likely perpetrators.

Having traced the origin of the call made to the Climax agency to the payphone in the lobby of the Hollywood public library on Ivar Street, officers next scoured there for clues.

They were able to lift fingerprints from the payphone, but by itself, this wasn't going to be of much help: the killer's prints were there, but so were many, many others—and there was nothing to match them to.

Staff at the library, however, reported seeing a man in the lobby behaving suspiciously on the afternoon of the day Kim disappeared. They described him as tall, dark, and wearing a mustache. He had been seen by one of the library attendants lingering too long at the payphone. He had been speaking to someone on the payphone, had waited there, and had then received a call back. The parking lot attendant at the library also described seeing a man of the same description.

The killers were seen by another person that afternoon at the library.

Cheryl Burke was browsing in the library stacks when a bushy-haired man glared at her through a gap in the shelves. He pulled a menacing face at her, aping the boogie man, and she rapidly moved to another location. The man then appeared again around a corner, staring at her in a kind of sick game of peek-a-boo.

Unsurprisingly, Cheryl decided to cut her library visit short, and went to retrieve her car from the parking lot.

She saw the same man there again, this time in the company of a younger, taller man, with a mustache. As she backed her car out, she watched the men talking briefly, and then the younger man approached her car and glared at her as she sped away.

These details of Cheryl's encounter with the stranglers did not actually come out until much later, at trial. Had the police had her description of the mustachioed man in hand when they headed over to Tamarind to interview the residents, they might have handled things differently. Then again, maybe not.

The detectives verified that apartment 114 was unoccupied, having at that time not been under lease. It appeared to have been entered by an unsecured sliding glass door to the patio, but there were no other signs of disturbance. They lifted several sets of prints from doors and handles, but again, they didn't know where to look to find a match that would reveal the identity of the men they were seeking.

Rightly, they surmised that there was some kind of connection between the Tamarind Terrace Apartments and the killers; one or both of them may have lived there, either at the time or in the past, or they may have had a contact or associate in the apartment block.

This was potentially an important break in the case: a physical location that could be connected to the murders and maybe those that committed them. Additionally, Jane King had been abducted just down the street, at the corner of Tamarind and Franklin. The prudent course of action might have been to have given the highest priority and scrutiny to the process of interviewing the residents. But this isn't what happened.

The taskforce had taken over allocation of resources to the investigation, and the officers who were sent to Tamarind had not been engaged on any investigative work in connection with the previous murders, and knew little about the facts of the case to date.

They didn't know, for example, that a resident on the third floor of the Tamarind had in fact already come up in the investigation. Now was a time when it would have been useful for the contents of the Weckler notebook to have been studied and logged so it could be cross-referenced at a later time. But that hadn't happened either.

A number of residents told the detectives they had heard screams and a commotion between nine and ten the night of the murder, but they hadn't reported anything, because men beating their wives was a common occurrence in the block and it was regarded as a private matter.

Most of these "witnesses" were dirty and disheveled, unforthcoming, and acted like the whole thing was an inconvenience. So the cops were almost relieved when they got to speak with Mr. Kenneth Bianchi, a polite and well-spoken young man who invited them in, offered them coffee, and expounded with casual fervor on his respect and admiration for the police.

Now here was a man they could relate to. This Ken told the officers that he had recently participated in the ride-along program. This was a scheme in which civilians could learn about police operations by sitting in patrol cars. The stranglers were thought to be posing as police officers or to have some strong interest in policing. But no alarm bells rang. Bianchi's enthusiasm was instead seen as recommendation in his favor that diminished his chances of being a suspect.

The man's resemblance to the description provided by witnesses at the library—tall, with dark hair and a mustache—also did not set off any warnings in the minds of the detectives.

Bianchi was utterly convincing as the concerned civilian.

—These murders are just terrifying! It's just unbelievable what some people are capable of. You guys really have my utmost sympathies dealing with all this. It can't be easy.

When the officers asked him what, if anything, he had seen or heard that night, his answer squared with those given by many of the other residents.

—I thought there was some quarrel going on. A guy and his lady having a tiff. Happens all the time in this building.

As far as the detectives were concerned, everything checked out. They felt more positive about their interview with Bianchi than they did with those held with the other residents.

He was a good citizen. He wasn't the kind of guy to ignore someone in trouble. But when you lived in a dump like that, the same rules didn't really apply. Los Angeles was a big city. There were all kinds of people and all kinds of stuff going on. It was understandable why you might not want to get into someone else's business.

The interview hadn't been unpleasant, and the coffee was nice, but they hadn't learned anything useful either.

They went away confident that it, and all the others that day, had been just another waste of their time.

\* \* \*

In the following days, reporters flocked to the Tamarind Apartments to speak with the residents and get their own scoop on the story. One of these was a Mrs. Irene Weigel, who lived on the fourth floor and was the manager of the building.

She told reporters that a man had come to enquire about the vacant first floor apartment on the Monday, the day before Kimberly Martin was killed. She described him as being in his twenties, wearing blue jeans and a print shirt, with longish brown hair.

While showing the man the apartment she noticed the lights were off, and went into the other room to switch them on, leaving the man alone. She speculated that at that time he had unfastened the latch on the door to the patio.

After seeing the apartment, the man had left, saying—ironically, in hindsight—"I'll probably be back."

It seems inconceivable that the apartment manager, living on the fourth floor of the same block as Bianchi, did not know or recognize him when he came to view the apartment.

This opens a few possibilities: either the man who came to see the apartment was not Bianchi, or if it was Bianchi, Mrs. Weigel did not share this information with the police or the media. Or, they did not follow it up.

Raising more questions is the fact that some residents reported to the press that a man had been seen coming and going from apartment 114 for some time, and that he was not a resident of the complex. The *Times Daily* reported on 16 December that two former residents of the same block had earlier reported that a man had been seen using the supposedly vacant apartment 114 on and off for months, slipping into the building behind residents when they opened the outer doors, and entering the apartment through an unlocked patio door. They described him as long haired and mustachioed.

What is clear is that Bianchi was operating right under the noses of the investigators, hiding in plain sight as it were.

It is also obvious that the clues and leads now available should have all pointed in the direction of making continued surveillance of the Tamarind Apartments and further questioning of the residents there.

But again—it didn't happen.

*　*　*

Lois Lee, taking a more proactive stance than the investigators, decided to share with the press her story of her failed attempts to get the police's attention when Kimberly Martin went missing.

She was incensed by the callous response to the incident, the insinuation that the life of a prostitute was without value, and the apparent indifference to solving a case that should have been top of their priority list.

Lee had also been trying for months, without success, to get the police to speak with several women she knew who had information that she was sure was relevant to the case. Lee had access to particulars that indicated the Hillside Stranglers were pimps, and were currently or recently active in prostitution activities in Los Angeles.

Lee had had no cooperation from the police, but had the ear of several reporters. With their help she made an appearance on KNBC news.

In the segment, broadcast on national television, she stated: *If you are involved in the prostitution business and you think you know who the Hillside Strangler is and you don't want to talk to the police. Don't call them, call me.*

She then posted her home phone number on national TV, so people could directly dial their leads to her.

A public relations disaster for the Sheriff's department and the taskforce followed. About twenty women, a mix of social service and hotline representatives and feminist activists, gathered outside the Parker Center chanting with placards on the Thursday afternoon following the murder, protesting the failure of police to respond swiftly to Martin's disappearance.

When asked by reporters why they were there, picket organizer Beth Ingber bluntly told the reporters that the police considered prostitutes legitimate victims.

—We're protesting on behalf of all prostitutes—and all women.

This ruckus outside the taskforce headquarters was disruptive and embarrassing. The authorities swung into action to put out the fire.

City Councilman David Cunningham penned a letter to the President of the Police Commission requesting an investigation of the delay in questioning Lois Lee. The missive charged that investigators had failed to act quickly on numerous calls made by Lee and demanded that the Commission, as head of the Los Angeles Police Department, make enquiries and determine what steps needed to be taken to prevent any such "oversights" in the future.

LAPD spokesman Lieutenant Dan Cooke did little to quell all the negative publicity when he addressed these claims before the press.

—Finding out what happened isn't the top priority, he said. We've got eleven murders we're trying to solve.

The reply was frankly stunning, but it also reveals certain assumptions in the taskforce's thinking about these crimes. The statement gave away that the police, or at least many of them, did not think there was a relationship between attending to queries about a missing prostitute and solving the case. The same assumptions would seem to have been behind their repeated dismissal of Lee's requests to talk to prostitutes about information they had. Why was that?

It might have been because they thought there might be several stranglers on the loose. If all these murders weren't the work of the same guys, maybe the men who killed Yolanda Washington and Judy Miller weren't the same men who killed Kristina Weckler and Lauren Wagner.

Or maybe it was just the idea that the murder of a prostitute was a banal occurrence, part of the fabric of rough life in LA, whereas the murder of a young woman from a good family was freakish, abnormal and horrifying.

Really, the thinking—or the image of reality that the thinking tried to protect—was that these two worlds did not intersect. The press and the authorities tried to preserve the comforting illusion that respectable society and the criminal underworld operated separately, the former not contaminated by the latter.

But the reality of this case would put paid to that idea.

# Chapter 14

Weeks had passed. Women had died. Families were destroyed. The authorities made promise after promise, but they were still no closer to arresting the Hillside Strangler. Public frustration mounted. And now questions were asked.

The Los Angeles *Herald Examiner* spoke aloud the thoughts of many:

"Why can't the Los Angeles Police Department, which is considered one of the best in the world, solve the Hillside Strangler murder case?"

Around the same time, the Los Angeles Times published a 60,000-word special supplement on the LAPD. The Hillside Strangler case was not the topic under discussion, but surely provided the context in which the report was to be received. The editorial criticized the department for sloppy investigative work, failure to follow through on arrests and interview witnesses, its undistinguished conviction rate and it's less than desirable relations with the district attorney's office.

The LAPD and taskforce continually defended themselves against attacks on their competence by pointing to the staggering amount of information they had to sift through in connection with the case.

Unfortunately the information overload turning their investigation into the search for the proverbial pin in a haystack was generated not only by a panic-stricken community, but by the police themselves.

In desperation for a break they had widened their nets, looking at cases far outside the areas where the abduction and dumping sites were concentrated. The locations were centered on the areas between Hollywood, Glendale and the county border to the north; but with the freeway system giving the killers access to the whole city, the detectives became uncertain of where to draw the boundaries in their investigation.

The taskforce now decided to pull and review the files on every unsolved murder of a female in the past two years in the wider Los Angeles area, in locations as far away as Bakersfield. Certainly, they were desperate to get their hands on a viable lead. But part of the motivation was to provide reassurance, to be seen to be "doing something" even if in reality they were far from their goal.

And, if police made arrests in any cases of strangled women, of which there were many in Los Angeles that fall and winter, they could briefly claim success in detaining a suspect in the Hillside case, even if the victim had fallen prey to a different killer altogether.

As it happened, the latter half of December 1977, and the month of January 1978, was a quiet time for the stranglers. Maybe they had been spooked by how close they had come to being caught with the Kimberly Martin murder. Either way, they were in a lull, but the police and public did not realize this; they continued to misattribute fresh killings of young women in and around Los Angeles to the Hillside Strangler.

Margaret Madrid, seven years old, had been left alone for five minutes on a Saturday afternoon at the corner of Temple Avenue and Amar Road in West Covina, while her sister went into a grocery store. She was later found in a gutter on 6 November in the city of Industry, in the San Gabriel region. This area is adjacent to the northeast suburbs where many of the Hillside victims were found. Press reports citing police information linked her murder with the Hillside Stranglers.

Nobody found out what really happened to Margaret until some fifteen years later, and the solving of her murder was entirely accidental. Police discovered a manuscript penned by an incarcerated killer who was going under the nom de plume of John Novak.

John Novak's real name was Manuel Cortez. He had been convicted of killing two eleven-year-old girls up in Oregon, and imprisoned in the state penitentiary in Salem, where he was working on the manuscript to while away the empty hours. Despite his only being convicted in relation to the Oregon killings, detectives knew that Cortez was also active around San Gabriel in the late seventies.

With the help of a collaborator on the outside, Cortez had pitched the manuscript—a kind of diary of a serial killer, purporting to be fiction—to a handful of interested publishers. The police seized a copy of the manuscript from the collaborator's home and uncovered within it details of several unsolved cases going back to the seventies, including that of Margaret Madrid.

Detective Les Rainey of the Eugene, Oregon Police Department said that the simultaneous presence of the Hillside Stranglers in the northeast of the city had always complicated the investigation of Cortez's San Gabriel murders. There was a fair amount of confusion about which unsolved cases might be linked to them, and which to Cortez.

Therese Berry was another name linked to the Hillside Strangler in November 1977. Nineteen-year old Berry was found raped and strangled on 4 November in Walnut, in the far-east corner of the greater Los Angeles area and a separate county. This was a considerable distance from the primary locations where Hillside victims were found, but near Industry, where Madrid's body was discovered.

A Joseph Conrad Humphries was charged and convicted with her murder in 1981. Humphries had been hired by Loran Berry, Therese Berry's husband, to carry out the murder so that he could collect on a life insurance policy he had taken out on his wife. The primary motive was pecuniary gain; the rape of Ms. Berry was a collateral "perk" Humphries has seized the opportunity for in carrying out the murder, which confused the police.

As if the numbers of strangling murders of women and girls all over Los Angeles wasn't enough to confuse the investigators, some of the murders were thought to be copycat killings, actually designed to look like the work of the Hillside Strangler.

In a case attracting such a level of publicity, copycat slayings had to be considered a possibility, as distasteful as it was. Individuals who commit copycat crimes are usually severely disturbed, their deeds provoked by massive media attention given to high-profile cases which saturate the culture. Sometimes, however, the motive is more sinister.

Carolyn Williams, twenty-one years old, and Paula Ward, eighteen, were murdered during the Christmas weekend of 1977. William's partially nude, strangled body was found in a parking lot in the Wiltshire district, and Ward was found on the same day at the Rose Bowl, Pasadena. Police arrested Thomas Davis, 24, and Stephen d'Orsey Devezin, 40, in connection with the murders. The two men were traced via a license number plate to a motel where an employee reported witnessing a man carrying what appeared to be a body wrapped in a blanket to a car.

The investigating Pasadena police thought they had cracked the Hillside Strangler case and immediately set up a liaison with the taskforce. But there were glaring dissimilarities in the Williams/Ward murders and the other cases. For one thing, Davis and Devezin were black, and eyewitness accounts thus far pointed to Caucasian perpetrators in the Hillside cases. Additionally, Williams and Ward had not been sexually assaulted.

Davis and Devezin were quickly ruled out as suspects in the Hillside cases, but Daryl Gates publicly alluded to the possibility that Williams and Ward had been killed out of some perverse desire to help throw the police off the trail of the real killers, describing the two slayings in press releases as copycat murders to "lay blame on someone else".

On the heels of this latest fiasco, failure to make progress in the case was increasingly blamed on dissension in the ranks. The headlines had a repetitive tenor:

"Strangler investigation hampered by a bevy of problems"

"Fighting among cops hampers death probe"

The different departments involved in the investigation could not agree on which bodies were linked to the stranglers, or what—and how much—information should be given to the media and the public.

Symbolic of the confusion, LAPD Commander William Booth again publicly declined to rule out any of the victims with the exception of Ward and Williams as targets of the same killer, or to pinpoint any as connected. Coroner's investigators were part of the taskforce but disagreed with police about what details should be given out. Tensions between the Glendale and Los Angeles departments rose when Glendale Police Chief Duane Baker made a casual remark at a civic gathering about the sexual nature of the crimes. These details had been largely withheld from the public to permit more informative grilling of suspects.

By Christmas 1977, despite the police's reservations about definitively connecting the many strangling cases in Los Angeles that fall and winter, press reports routinely counted the death toll of the Hillside Strangler at 12 or 13 victims. The true toll at that point was in fact nine, but with the community under the impression that the rampage was continuing and even escalating, and so much negative publicity about their handling of the case, there was more pressure than ever on the police to clamp down on suspects.

On 8 February 1978, the police announced that they might have a lead on a viable contender.

Earlier, on 19 January, Daryl Gates had publicly requested that the stranglers come forward and surrender themselves. Then, like manna from heaven, a letter arrived at Mayor Tom Bradley's office, postmarked 19 January, claiming to be authored by the Hillside Strangler.

*Dear Mr. Mayor—PLEASE!! Lisson to me. I am very sick but I do not want to go back to that place. I hate that place. My mother told me to kill those bad and evil ladys. It's not my fault. My mother makes my head hurt that's why I kill her but I can't get her out of my head she keeps comin' back.*

This opening gives a good teaser of the rest, six pages of substantially incoherent rambling, scratched by hand in a looping, childish script with pencil.

The writer offered to turn himself and his accomplice into the mayor's office in exchange for assurances of his safety, implying that if authorities did not act in response to the letter and provide safe haven, the strangler would strike again.

Gates immediately convened a press conference. His press release carefully hedged bets between declaring a victory and not saying much at all. There was nothing to prove the letter was really from the Hillside Strangler, but they were taking it seriously. He then dropped the bombshell that the letter contained a detail that, if verified, would prove the letter's author was the Hillside Strangler.

The detail Gates referred to was an object the writer apparently had in his possession. Gates would not disclose what the object was, but told assembled reporters that if the writer did have it, "we would be inclined to believe he really is the killer."

Public assurances were then given that the letter had been examined by the taskforce, and the decision to hold the news conference had been made with the approval of the police.

But the story behind the scenes at the Parker Center was rather different. Several taskforce officers were angered by the public release of the letter, because they felt quite strongly that it was a hoax. After all, based on observation of his crimes, there had been nothing to suggest so far that the Hillside Strangler was demented, confused, or intellectually challenged.

Nothing in the letter suggested the author had any knowledge of the murders beyond what had been reported in the media, and there was little to no chance, they thought, that the real perpetrator would be inclined to turn himself in—especially in response to a public appeal by the police.

It later emerged that the author of the letter was a severely disturbed mental patient who had escaped from an institution. He had been confined in a hospital after murdering his mother as a child—facts vaguely alluded to, as we have seen, in the letter itself. His mother used an oxygen tank, and the child had severed the tubing, killing her in her sleep. The man was terrified of returning to the hospital so contacted the Mayor's office with the false confession, begging to be taken into alternative custody. He was deemed to be a danger to himself, but likely not others.

It also came out that some members of the press already knew the identity of the man, because he had haunted locations where Hillside victims were dumped and told reporters, and anyone else handy who would listen, that he was the Hillside Strangler and he was going to turn himself into the mayor. The reporters knew the man was nothing more than a whacko, not the strangler; but they didn't try to get him help, get him off the streets, or alert the police.

* * *

When this promising lead didn't pan out, instead turning into another public relations clusterfuck, the police decided to move the public's attention on with the announcement on 19 February of another "viable suspect".

"Only in Los Angeles", people would later say about the attempt to put thirty-seven-year-old actor Ned York forward as the Hillside Strangler.

It was almost too perfect. Not only was York a Hollywood entertainer, he was best known for his performances on a cop show, the popular and long running *Starsky and Hutch*. Police had received a rambling telephone call from York in which he relayed that he had information about the Hillside murders, and they brought him in for questioning.

During the interview a tearful and agitated York became completely incoherent before falling asleep. The explanation for his erratic behavior was drugs, a common problem amongst Hollywood actors. York was a cocaine addict and was also in the midst of a marriage breakdown. Trying to blow off some steam, he went on a PCP bender, during which he comprehensively unraveled and called the police. He later explained his false confession as a misguided cry for help.

## A City Owned

The cops never genuinely thought York had anything to do with the case from the moment they brought him in. But since he had confessed, they decided to publicize his arrest and get some of the heat off.

This episode effectively finished Ned York's acting career. A remorseful York told the papers in May 1978 that he had been dumped by friends, dropped by his agent, and forced onto unemployment benefits. He always wanted to be famous, he said, but not infamous. It sure wasn't some ill-conceived publicity stunt. Who the hell would want that kind of publicity?

\* \* \*

The arrest of Ned York was not the first time the worlds of serial murder and Hollywood would meet in the chronicle of the stranglers.

Catharine Lorre Baker was born under an unlucky star. Orphaned at seventeen when her mother died unexpectedly, she had lost her father five years earlier. A sufferer of juvenile diabetes, her life was filled with chronic pain and medical treatments for associated conditions, many unsuccessful.

But she did have one thing that stood in her favor. Her father, the one who had died when she was eleven, was actor Peter Lorre. She was therefore, by accident, blessed with a small degree of fame and public esteem herself.

One night in 1977, Catharine, then twenty-five, was travelling on foot in downtown Los Angeles to meet her husband, who had just got off work. At the corner of Highland and Hawthorne, a blue Cadillac swerved and screeched to a stop in front of her, blocking the road.

Catharine stepped back as two men got out of the car and walked towards her. Showing her what looked like a police badge, they demanded her identification.

Catharine was carrying her citizenship papers and showed them to the "cops". The papers stated that her name was Catharine Lorre and that she had been born in Hamburg, Germany in 1953. Listed as her father was Peter Lorre, film actor.

The younger of the two men, who had previously addressed Catharine in the most abrupt and chilly manner, suddenly became very friendly and conversational, as if they were old friends chatting over a drink. Smiling and tapping his index finger on the photograph, he asked, is that *the* Peter Lorre?

—Oh yes, said Catharine.

She pulled an old photograph out of her purse and gave it to the cop. In the photo, a little Catharine was sitting on the knee of Peter Lorre wearing the distinctive moonish face that identified the actor all over the world.

—No kidding. It really is Peter Lorre! Hey, Tony, we got Peter Lorre's daughter here!

The other officer perused the photo.

—Well I'll be. What are the chances?

The two were excited, like little kids, and started comparing their favorite moments from Lorre's films as if Catharine wasn't even there.

Peter Lorre originally hailed from Austria and was first made famous for playing a serial killer and child rapist in the German film of 1931, *M*. In later years he moved to California and played several roles as murderers and monsters in crime and horror films for Warner Brothers and Roger Corman.

The two "cops" were great fans of his work.

—Well, they said to Catherine, you better get going now—and be careful, you shouldn't be out walking alone at night you know, it isn't safe.

Catharine Lorre had just had an encounter with the Hillside Stranglers. The only reason she was alive was because she was Peter Lorre's daughter, but she continued on her way to meet her husband, none the wiser.

# Chapter 15

All their crank leads might have bought the police some time before the eyes of the public, but behind the scenes they were getting desperate for a genuine break in the case. That desperation led them to consider options they normally wouldn't.

There had been all kinds of offers of help from psychics, psychiatrists and private detectives. They were skeptical about the potential value of many of these offers but they also realized that, at this point, they maybe needed to think outside the box. A letter arrived at the LAPD from a private detective from Germany promising he could solve the case for the price of an air ticket. Bob Grogan could not pronounce the man's name, and instead jokingly referred to him as "Dr. Shickelgruber". That gives a general idea of the seriousness with which the private detective was regarded.

"Dr. Schickelgruber" in fact wrote several times. Grogan responded to his letters, keeping up a kind of desultory correspondence mostly out of amusement and curiosity, but he never took up his offer to fly out to Los Angeles.

The German detective, however, was determined. He eventually travelled to Los Angeles of his own volition and arrived on the LAPD's doorstep demanding an audience.

He gave the following description of the suspects they should be looking for:
*Two Italians. Might be brothers. Around thirty-five years of age.*

Grogan had no way to evaluate this seemingly random assessment. The German did not speak English very well, and due to the language barrier, he could not clearly communicate how he had arrived at his theory. Grogan was unimpressed and summarily dismissed him.

Of course, "Dr. Shickelgruber" turned out to be uncannily close.

In 1977 and 1978, when the Hillside murders were going on, the FBI Behavioral Sciences Unit was in its relative infancy. Established in 1972, it was there that the term "serial killer" was invented, and where the science of criminal profiling was developed. Nobody can be sure how the Berlin detective came to his conclusions, however it seems possible that he had had some—perhaps simply intuitive—grasp of profiling techniques.

Had the LAPD taken seriously the assertion that the killers were Italian, a few simple steps would have led them straight to their man. If the detectives could have surmised that they were looking for an Italian resident at the Tamarind Apartments, where Kimberly Martin was lured to her death, or at the East Garfield Avenue apartments—Kristina Weckler's residence and last known whereabouts before she was killed—a check of past tenant records would have revealed Kenneth Bianchi was one of the men they were looking for.

A panel of psychiatrists and psychologists whose opinions were solicited for an article in the *Los Angeles Times* had their own theories about what kind of man the police should be hunting. Their opinions regurgitated the stereotype of the criminal as an anti-social loner, a creature whom society had failed to successfully integrate.

The Hillside Strangler was thought to be white and in his late twenties or early thirties. He was unmarried, either single or divorced—in any case "definitely not living with a woman".

He was probably unemployed or subsisted on short-term casual employment—problems with authority would prevent him holding onto a job too long. He was "passive, cold and manipulative—all at once". He probably already had a rap sheet for minor offences. He came from a broken home marred by cruelty, especially at the hands of women, presumably the mother. Like all psychopathic murderers he will have wet the bed, tortured animals and set things on fire as a child or adolescent. It was generally agreed he did not enjoy normal sex. The killing itself was the source of sexual gratification. Possibly he was a necrophile—the enjoyment came in having sex with a woman after he had killed her.

Dr. Louis Jolyon West, Chairman of Psychiatry and Behavioral Sciences at UCLA and Director of that university's Neuropsychiatry Institute, rejected the "team killers" theory. He believed the strangler was a man living on the periphery of society whom nobody would suspect. He enjoyed the thrill of danger and thought himself invincible. Only homosexuals killed in teams, he asserted.

Some of the profiles were on the right track, but too vague to be of any use in finding the killers. White guys with patchy employment records who hated their mothers were a dime a dozen, in Los Angeles or anywhere else. There was a certain naivety in the theorizing that was probably the same cause of the police failing to look too closely at certain suspects and situations. The Hillside Strangler was assumed to be totally aberrant, a creature shunned by normal society, stalking on the fringes. This was far from the truth.

Attempts at physical profiling were more on point. The taskforce had engaged a forensic artist to put together a series of composite drawings of their suspects drawn from the various witness statements.

There were certain constants and themes that recurred in the physical descriptions. Both men had very dark hair, towards the black end of the color spectrum. It was thought possible that they were of Latin or Mediterranean ethnic background; the older one had been described more than once as being of Puerto-Rican appearance. Just about everyone had mentioned his bushy mop of curly hair and said he had an olive complexion. The younger one however had fair skin. He was often described as wearing a mustache and he had acne scars on his lower face.

The forensic artist was not yet aware that his drawing had in fact produced an extremely good likeness of one of the men they were looking for. The man stared from the drawing with intense, penetrating eyes. The facial structure was somewhat long and angular, with a fine, straight nose.

The only confusion seemed to be around the hair. The artist had drawn the same face several times with different hairstyles: some short and close-cropped, others long and wavy.

This stealthy predator of the American wildlife was most creative in his tactics of camouflage.

# Chapter 16

Christmas came and went without incident. Then it was a new year. 1978. New years incline people towards hope, and the frail optimism that things can get better, that they can start anew.

But on 16 February 1978, it happened again. Jan Sims, a middle-aged schoolteacher at the Heritage School in Glendale, was driving her car along Riverside Drive in Burbank when she saw a man trying to pull a girl into his car.

It was around noon on a clear sunny day, but even that did not deter them. They were right there, in broad daylight, with more than the odd car and pedestrian passing by.

The man—mid-forties, slender but wirily strong—had the girl by the arms. She had been waiting for a bus, and he was pulling her away from the bus stop, towards an Excalibur pulled up to the curb. His associate was waiting in the vehicle. Jan saw him too, but less distinctly.

Mrs. Sims wasn't afraid of some nasty man. She stepped straight out of her car and walked towards him, waving her finger, scolding him like one of her students:

—You leave her alone! Get away from her this instant! I'll call the police!

Startled, the man released the girl's arms, and she fell gratefully into Mrs. Sims', her cries of fear turning to cries of relief.

He was furious. Who did this old bag think she was, throwing him off his game and interrupting their plans?

As Jan bundled the girl into her car he fixed her with an irate stare and threw an unusual parting shot which Mrs. Sims would later include in her report to the police:

*God will get you for this!*

Mrs. Sims comforted the girl for a while before putting her safely on a bus home. It was sometime after that she realized she had never learned the girl's name. But she kept replaying the incident in her mind, and was troubled enough by it she decided she had to report it to the police.

Once she had gathered her thoughts, she grew increasingly sure she had just circumvented a kidnapping attempt by the Hillside Strangler. Had she not just happened to have been there, in the right place at the right time, that girl would probably be dead.

Over at the North Hollywood station, she told the police as much, but they weren't having a bar of it. Like cops all over Los Angeles, the officers there were accustomed to receiving masses of such tips from hysterical citizens.

*Oh, sure, the Hillside Strangler*, they would say, having the concerned citizen fill out some paperwork to be filed away and never looked at again. *He's everywhere these days...*

The officer who received Mrs. Sims' report didn't believe her, and thought she was either making it up, or hadn't actually seen what she thought she saw.

What were the chances these guys would try to pick up a girl off a busy street in the middle of the day? He told Mrs. Sims to go home, put her feet up and relax. He'd file her report with all the other supposed sightings of the strangler.

The following week, Mrs. Sims tried to engage the police again. She telephoned the North Hollywood station to report that she had seen the same car, the Excalibur, parked along Colorado Street in Glendale.

The officer who responded to the call was annoyed that Mrs. Sims had taken it upon herself to pester the police again. They had real work to get on with. He told her he would file a report to go with her original statement, and that was that.

Having been dismissed twice, Mrs. Sims didn't think it was worth contacting the cops again to let them know that, now she thought about it, she had seen one of the two men in the Excalibur on another occasion.

A few weeks before the attempted kidnapping of the girl at the bus stop, Mrs. Sims had been parked in a lot on Lankershim in the Valley.

She was waiting for her daughter, who she was picking up from work. One of the two men—the younger, taller one, with pockmarked skin—was hanging around in the parking lot. On that occasion he was wearing a dark three-piece suit and carrying a briefcase. He had noticed Mrs. Sims watching him, walked over to her car and, through the window, asked her what she was doing there.

After Ms. Sims explained that she was waiting for her daughter, the man had said he was "just checking" because he was responsible for security in the building. Mrs. Sims had remembered the incident because something about the man had made her feel very uneasy. She didn't believe his story about his being security personnel. In fact, while the man seemed to be somehow accusing her of "loitering", that's exactly what she felt he was doing.

Had Mrs. Sims felt confident to relay this information to the police, and had they taken it seriously, they would have got their guy. A check of individuals associated with that building would have revealed Bianchi's name, and his prints would have matched those taken from the payphone at the Hollywood library, and the apartment at 1950 Tamarind.

As it was, Mrs. Sims was so put off by her experience dealing with the police that she never contacted them again.

A few hours after she rescued the girl on Riverside, twenty-year old Cindy Lee Hudspeth, the tenth victim of the Hillside Stranglers, was dead.

Mrs. Sims had indeed intercepted an attempted abduction; and the two men would try their luck again later the same day, this time with success.

None of this background to the Hudspeth murder would be known until much later.

On the afternoon of February 17, the day after she disappeared, Salerno was called out to the hills of Los Angeles Crest, just past the Glendale-Pasadena line. A forest service worker piloting a chopper in the area spotted a sedan crashed in a ravine. Rescue workers went to investigate further, and discovered Cindy's nude body crammed into the trunk.

* * *

Like most people, once you scratched the surface, she wasn't easily categorized. She was devoutly Christian. A bible school teacher, conservative in her social mores. A very careful person, her mother and boss would later say.

But Cindy loved disco dancing, and was very good at it. She had recently won an award in a competition, and was considering giving lessons, but she didn't want to invite strangers into her home. That was because she was deathly afraid of the Hillside Strangler. She was even considering moving back into her mother's house, to be safer.

Cindy also loved her car, a newish, smart-looking Datsun, bright orange. On the afternoon of 16 February, she was headed to Glendale Community College, where she worked part-time as a clerk. But she decided, on impulse, to stop along the way, and get some new floor mats for the car.

Her apartment, oddly enough, was on East Garfield Avenue, just across from the complex Kristina Weckler had lived in.

But the stranglers didn't get her at her home. Cindy walked into the nest herself. After all, she would never have guessed that one of them was the respectable local businessman who had given her a card at the Robin Hood Inn, when she was waitressing there.

Cindy left her place between four-thirty and five. Her roommate, Michele Exner—the last to see her—confirmed this timeline with police. She got into her car, drove down East Garfield and turned onto Colorado Street, which is along the route to Glendale College.

Cindy was profoundly unlucky. On the afternoon she decided to stop in at the trim shop on Colorado Street, Kenneth Bianchi happened to be visiting with his partner in crime, the owner of the business, the same store that Yolanda Washington had visited with her friend Deborah Noble.

The decision to kill Cindy was made then and there. It passed silently between the two men in a glance that she probably did not even notice.

Cindy's disappearance came to the attention of the authorities quickly, because her boss raised the alarm when she failed to arrive for work that same afternoon. None of this could help her situation though.

Still several steps behind their targets, the cops had no idea there was any connection between the murders and the popular auto upholstery business on Colorado Street. They did, at least, notice the connection between Cindy's place of residence and the Weckler murder. They decided this time to thoroughly check things out at Cindy's apartment block on East Garfield Avenue.

Unfortunately it was a matter of the right approach for the wrong occasion. The investigation at East Garfield sent the cops on a wild goose chase. Cindy's neighbor Betty Joseph told them that Cindy had had a "surprise visitor" on the afternoon she disappeared. At around four-thirty, Betty reported that she had heard Cindy call out to somebody: *What are you doing here?*

Mrs. Joseph said Cindy didn't sound disturbed exactly, more surprised; it was as if whoever had arrived at her door was a friend she wasn't expecting, or hadn't seen for a long time.

The initial theory was that Cindy, like Kimberly Martin, had been abducted by someone in the apartment block, perhaps someone she knew. The detectives questioned everyone there in detail. In the process, they learned that Betty Joseph had been mistaken. The voice she had heard calling out did not belong to Cindy, but to another resident.

Out at Angeles Crest, they were derailed by another false lead. Two men in a yellow van had been spotted by the forest service chopper pilot in the nearby area shortly after he discovered Cindy's orange Datsun dumped over the side of the embankment. In this case, once press reports appeared stating that police were looking for two men and a yellow van, the driver of the van contacted police and identified himself as a forest service officer.

A more promising tip came from a potential witness who came forward after press reports detailed the location of the dumped Datsun. Janice Ackers told police that on the evening of 16 February, she had been driving along the Angeles Crest Highway when she had noticed a car approaching very fast behind her. She then saw that there was another car directly behind it. As she stopped to make a left turn, the first car, which she described as a red-orange sedan, sped past her, and the driver stared at her through the window. She said the man had a dark beard, and a wild, crazy look in his eyes.

The beard didn't jibe with what other witnesses had seen, but it was possible one of the men had grown a beard since those earlier sightings. Their suspect Kenneth Bianchi was in fact a chameleon who altered his appearance frequently by changing the way he wore his hair. Sometimes he wore a mustache, sometimes he was clean-shaven. Sometimes he wore his hair cropped close, sometimes he wore it long. At times it looked straight, at other times it appeared curly or waved.

Everything else in Ms. Acker's report, particularly the description of the car, which sounded like Cindy's Datsun, seemed to fit. If her account was to be believed, and she had actually seen the stranglers that evening and not some other men, the killers had abducted Cindy, murdered her, and then one of them had driven her car—with her body in the trunk—to Angeles Crest, with his accomplice following in another car behind. Together they had pushed her car over the cliff, and then left together in the other vehicle.

The picture that was emerging from questioning of the residents at the apartment complex suggested that Cindy had run into trouble after she left.

There were no signs of struggle or forced entry at Cindy's apartment, and aside from Betty Joseph, nobody had seen or heard anything unusual.

Cindy's route to the college, located at Glendale Avenue, would have taken her down Colorado Street. The detectives concluded that she had been abducted somewhere between the fairly short distance between her apartment and the college; possibly—even probably—on Colorado.

Based on the abduction and dumping locations of the Hillside victims, Grogan and Salerno had for some time entertained the notion that one or both of the killers probably lived in the Glendale area. All of this seemed further confirmation of that. Grogan had in fact taken a map to Frank one day, which he had marked up with red pen, joining the dots of all the dump sites. The upholstery trim shop on Colorado was right in the middle of the circle—but because they didn't know what they were looking for, they just couldn't see it.

Finally, they were getting closer, forming a clearer picture of the type of men they were looking for, and where they probably lived.

What they didn't know is that they would never get the opportunity to solve the case. The few good leads they had would grow cold, and the killers would provide no new ones.

After the murder of Cindy Hudspeth, their Los Angeles rampage suddenly, and mysteriously, came to an end.

# Chapter 17

The warmer days came to California. A month passed; then two; then three. Los Angeles waited for news of another victim, but it never came. Homicide was the daily reality it had always been, but the bizarre and terrifying spate of stranglings that fall, and winter seemed to have come to an end.

Slowly, the city released a collective sigh, as the people allowed themselves to entertain the possibility that it might be over; and then, finally accepted that it really was.

This was a gradual process, not conscious, almost imperceptible. It took the form of simply moving onto new things.

The restless, futuristic nature of Californians came to the fore. The Dodgers won the National League and were going to the World Series. Los Angeles had just been announced as the city to host the 1984 Olympics. There was much to look forward to, or perhaps people were just forgetful.

Either way, the difference was incredible. The city was transformed, the streets alive again. Women walked the strips and malls, alone or in small groups, going about their business as if fear had never ruled. They stepped out of their homes confidently, no longer afraid to brave the outdoors without the protection of a man or a concealed weapon.

Salerno sometimes thought there was a fine line between looking on the bright side, and a certain deadness he observed around him, an insensitivity. That year Roman Polanski skipped bail on child sex charges of the vilest kind, escaping punishment by ditching Los Angeles for France. But Polanski was still the epitome of brilliance, everyone praised him and paid buckets to see his films. The mass suicide in Guyana, the so-called Jonestown Massacre, had resulted in the largest loss of civilian life on record. Everyone was shocked at first, but then it was just onto the next.

As for the Hillside Strangler, as far as the media were concerned, he was yesterday's story. He reappeared in the papers occasionally, like an abscess flaring. Two men were arrested when they were found to be dressed in Highway Patrol uniforms when they were stopped for a traffic violation. The cops questioned them at length, but they were quickly ruled out as suspects.

Another false win was declared when a woman named Roxanne Barnwell gunned down 37-year-old Richard Reynolds. Reynolds had been dressed as a police officer when he tried to abduct Ms. Barnwell in the Glendale area. All of this seemed such a perfect fit for who they were looking for, but the cops were wrong again, misled by the twisted inclinations of certain Los Angeles men.

Finally, in November 1978, the papers ran a number of stories on the Hillside Stranglers—this time to ponder where the killers had gone. A typical headline asked: "Hillside Strangler: Vanished? Dead? Or just lying low?"

While the city had largely moved on, the authorities were privately troubled by the cooling case, and this same question bothered them greatly. A year after the peak of the madness, the investigation was winding down, and even though the killers had never been caught, they were moving their resources elsewhere. The taskforce was still in operation, but had been reduced to twenty officers from the twelve dozen that had been manning the operation a year earlier, and had been moved into a smaller room of the Parker Center. Citizens still dialed in the odd tip, but effectively the leads were drying up.

They were working on the assumption that the Hillside Strangler was no longer a public threat. That assumption was a gamble, but with all that had been poured into the case and the lack of progress made, it was the easiest—and least embarrassing—course of action.

As it happened, the information they needed to solve the case was right at their fingertips, and at least as far back as March 1978, one of their suspects was equally within their grasp.

In late February 1978, two men who lived in a house on Corona Drive, Glendale, contacted the local PD with a tip. They said their former housemate, Kenneth Bianchi, was in possession of a California Highway Patrol badge. They were suspicious, because they knew Ken wasn't a policeman, and they thought he was "generally pretty strange". They had thrown Ken out for failure to pay rent, and they weren't sure where he was living now.

The Glendale officers checked motor registry information and connected Bianchi to an apartment at Verdugo Road, Glendale, where they sought him out for interview. The Glendale officer asked him if he had, or had ever had, a police badge.

Nah, answered Bianchi, as if the question was ridiculous. A smile, a small wave of the hand. He would have liked to have been a police officer, he said, but he had moved into real estate instead.

Ken struck the officer as far too clean-cut to be involved in criminality. He was polite, almost obsequious. There was a star struck, almost naïve quality about him as he talked with the officer about his respect for the police. Bluntly, he seemed like too much of a dork to be a crook. The detective took him at his word, and left.

Meanwhile, over at the LAPD headquarters, another tip had come in from a Mrs. Wanda Kellison. She told the detectives that her daughter Sheryl had been dating a strange young man named Kenneth Bianchi. Mrs. Kellison didn't like this Ken fellow one bit.

At this, the officers smirked. They had received hundreds of similar tips from concerned mothers all over the county; it was a popular way to express disapproval of your daughter's romantic choices, to call in and say your daughter was dating the Hillside Strangler.

Mrs. Kellison said she had argued with Sheryl several times about this young man. Wanda felt he was of poor character, largely because he was always borrowing money off Sheryl. But there was something just generally very off about him. He made her uncomfortable. And he was forever talking to Sheryl about the Hillside Strangler case.

Sheryl would have none of her mother's misgivings: she was devoted to her lover. It worried Wanda enough that she had decided to call the police.

Two LAPD officers, neither of them directly involved in the investigation, performed some quick checks on Bianchi. They traced him to his former residence at 809 East Garfield. The East Garfield address didn't jostle any gray matter, even though two of the victims, Kristina Weckler and Cindy Hudspeth, had lived on the very same street. And when they entered Bianchi's name into PATRIC, the so-called "Pattern Recognition" computer, the record of the prior interview at Tamarind did not appear.

The officers had already blandly concluded they were chasing another dud lead, but they headed over to 809 East Garfield anyway.

## A City Owned

There, the landlord praised Bianchi—who had since moved out of the complex—to the skies, describing him as a perfect tenant. So polite and helpful. You don't find many young men like him these days, he said. Another young female tenant had complained about Bianchi, but she was a troublemaker anyway, so he didn't put any stock into it.

Ken was the friendly, social type: he had kept in touch. In fact the landlord could give them his new address, over on Verdugo Road.

When the officers finally found this young man whose fine reputation so preceded him, and told him his name had come up in the Hillside Strangler investigation, he ushered them in with words of reassurance that he was happy to help them in any way possible. He had been following the case in the papers. He knew what the officers had been dealing with. He was sympathetic to their struggle.

The detectives asked him a few basic questions. How long had he been in Los Angeles? Did he have any involvement in police work? Had he ever been in jail?

At the last question Bianchi gave an embarrassed laugh, as if the very thought was preposterous. He wasn't involved in police work, but he admired the police and had applied to the LAPD reserves.

Bianchi was so cooperative and friendly that they again dismissed him as a good suspect. They wrote up their report and filed it away, without checking his LAPD reserves application, which had his fingerprints that matched those taken from the Hollywood public library payphone and the apartment at 1950 Tamarind.

Manual indexing of the clues and activities of the police in connection with the case would have yielded better results than the system the taskforce had in place. Having been instilled with false confidence in the amazing deductive powers of the fifty-thousand-dollar computer, the detectives continued to bounce from one bungle to another while their suspect sat right under their nose.

Ken Bianchi had now been interviewed three times in connection with the case, and had been passed over as a suspect every time. At this point he could be entirely forgiven for thinking the police were straight up stupid. If they hadn't found him out now, they never would.

# Chapter 18

Despite the effective winding up of the investigation by the end of 1978, the public relations team tried to appear upbeat. Gates, who had recently been promoted to Chief of Police, still felt that his men would crack the case. Commander William Booth, the media spokesman, made much of the fact that the investigation was still active and "sharpening its focus". He said they were now in the process of really sorting wheat from chaff; what was a valuable lead versus what wasn't.

Frank Salerno didn't say anything about Gates but offered his own markedly contrasting opinion to the papers. He said they had no real tangible leads, and that there were as many theories about where the stranglers had gone as there were investigators.

While Gates and Booth were putting a good face on things, it seemed pretty clear that the detectives had drifted far from their objective. In the same breath as he stated his confidence that the killers would be caught, Booth admitted that the investigators had never known and still didn't know whether "all 13" killings were the work of one person or group.

The reality was that the murders were over, and so was the pressure on the police. They had been embarrassed by their failure to solve the case, but the trouble had passed, and now they could get on with something else.

Still, it was common sense in law enforcement that such killers rarely stop killing of their own accord. They either stop because they have been apprehended on another charge or because they have themselves been killed. Or, they only appear to stop because they have moved onto another area. It is likely that, amidst their relief that the horror in Los Angeles was over, the investigators had this possibility niggling at the back of their minds.

Salerno remained preoccupied with the case long after it had begun growing cold. Talk of it had been banned at his house, everyone had moved on at the unit, but his ruminations continued after dark in the private corners of his mind. He felt that he had let down the girls. The investigation had been a mess. And what's worse he was nagged by the possibility they were still out there, just biding their time.

—Do you think it's over Frank? Grogan asked him.

—Maybe … but these serial type murderers, they're like gophers. They can pop up somewhere else.

\* \* \*

Another serial killer active in the US in 1977 and 1978 was, of course, Ted Bundy. In 1978, Bundy was much in the national headlines when, after evading authorities in Washington and Utah, and escaping from prison in Colorado, he was finally arrested in Florida after breaking into the Chi Omega sorority house in Tallahassee, Florida, and murdering Lisa Levy and Margaret Bowman. The Bundy story was a powerful illustration of the fact that serial killers tend to spread the path of their destruction far and wide if they are not stopped.

If the Los Angeles authorities were wondering if the Hillside Strangler would resume his career in murder somewhere else, they wouldn't have to wait long to get their answer.

In January 1979, two more women were raped, strangled, and dumped, as Cindy Hudspeth had been, inside a car—nearly 2,000 kilometers from Los Angeles, in the town of Bellingham, Washington, twenty miles south of the Canadian border.

# PART THREE
# FRESH GROUND

# Chapter 19

The Pacific Northwest has a reputation for breeding murderers. John Douglas, the FBI profiler of Gary Ridgway, the so-called Green River Killer who was convicted in 2002 for the murders of 48 women in the Seattle-Tacoma area, called it "America's killing fields."

Ted Bundy, America's most notorious serial killer, grew up in Tacoma and murdered several women in Washington before moving on to Utah. John Allen Muhammad, the DC sniper, was a former Tacoma resident, and Robert Yates Jr., a former Air National Guard helicopter pilot and smelter worker who pleaded guilty in 2000 to murdering 13 women in Spokane, Walla Walla and Skagit counties, was Washington born and bred. Across the border in Canada, Robert William Pickton, the "Pig Farmer Killer" of Port Coquitlam, British Columbia, was convicted in 2007 of the murder of six women, and was charged in the deaths of an additional twenty in Vancouver. And Canada's most prolific serial killer, Clifford Olson, who murdered at least eleven teenagers—both girls and boys—in the early 1980s, also lived and operated around Vancouver, B.C. The thick dark forests provide excellent hiding places for bodies, the wild desolation offers protection from busybodies and cops, and the honor roll of infamy is long.

Somehow, in 1979, Kenneth Bianchi had turned up in this same region, where he was in such good company. He was even known to drink at the Waterfront Tavern, which in later years would earn a reputation as the bar where serial killers enjoy a quiet tipple. When the DC Sniper was arrested in 2002, a bartender named Wally told the press that not only had John Allen Muhammad been a regular there, but Ted Bundy and James Kinney too. A press mob descended on the quiet watering hole. The tavern's owner, Lynne Farmer, complained that all the negative publicity had hurt her business. She rejected a proposal by one of the patrons to cash in on the notoriety by naming their sandwiches after serial killers.

The Waterfront is located in Bellingham, a picturesque coastal fishing town of around 206,000 inhabitants sandwiched between snow-capped Mount Baker and Bellingham Bay. This little town, with its quirky mix of hippies, yuppies, militiamen, seafarers, American Indians and tramps, has been connected to at least four serial killers in the last forty years. Even so, its bad reputation is probably undeserved. Bellingham isn't a magnet for criminals, but many might end up there on route to Canada and Alaska. Then and now, it is a quiet and safe community with an average of one to two homicides each year.

In 1979, the population of Bellingham was about one hundred thousand, and its relatively small size, and the rareness of crime, meant that the strangling deaths of two co-eds from Washington State University came as a massive shock to the community.

On the morning of 12 January 1979, the Bellingham PD received a call from the security office of Western Washington University. Two of their students, roommates Diane Wilder, age 27, from Bremerton, and Karen Mandic, 22, from Bellevue, Washington, were missing.

Violent crime was so unusual in Bellingham at the time that Police Chief Terry Mangan's first thought was that the two women had probably just left town on vacation without telling anyone. Upon retracing Karen Mandic's final whereabouts, however, he began to sense something was amiss.

Karen had last been seen at 7:00pm on Thursday, 11 January, when she left the Fred Meyer Department store where she worked part-time as a cashier. She was supposed to return at nine to help pack up and do the evening stock take. Karen was a very reliable employee, and her boss was alarmed when she failed to return without a word.

The manager phoned Steve Hardwick, a personal friend of Karen's, and explained that Karen had never come back to work. Hardwick was suspicious. Earlier in the week, Karen told him that she had been offered a job for that Thursday evening housesitting for a Dr. Catlow who was away on vacation with his family. The job had been offered to her not by Dr. Catlow himself, but by a security officer with the Whatcom Security Agency (WSA), a local company that provided mobile and static patrols in and around Bellingham. Hardwick thought the arrangement sounded iffy, because the security officer had pledged Karen to secrecy. It appeared that she had been engaged "off the books."

Karen had told Hardwick that the burglar alarm at Dr. Catlow's house was broken, and she was simply to mind the place for a couple of hours until the repair people arrived, after which she would return to work at Fred Meyer. Hardwick had advised Karen not to accept the job, because it didn't sound legitimate; but she had insisted, being excited about the prospect of easy money.

Karen had reassured Hardwick that everything would be fine; she was bringing her friend Diane Wilder along for company, and she knew the security guard: he had previously worked for security at Fred Meyer, and his new employer WSA was a very reputable company. She didn't mention that the guy had asked Karen for a date; actually, he had asked her several times.

Upon receiving the call from Karen's boss, Hardwick immediately drove to the Bayside address of Dr. Catlow, which he found deserted. He could not remember the security guard's name, but he did remember WSA, so he called them to ask for the details of the job Karen had been engaged on. Personnel at WSA examined their books, and the name Kenneth Bianchi came up in connection with the Bayside residence. He had been assigned to a job there, but the housesitting arrangement he had made with Karen was off the record. WSA realized that Bianchi had engaged someone on an unofficial job, and weren't happy about it.

Until that point, WSA thought Mr. Bianchi was a fine employee: he wasn't a Bellingham native, but he was friendly and pleasant, carrying out his duties with no apparent issues. But when, after receiving the call from Hardwick, they performed a belated background check on him, they were shocked at what they discovered.

Bellingham was a small town: the kind of place where people knew each other, and knew each other's business. Randy Moa, co-owner of WSA, spoke to a local woman named Susan Bird who was acquainted with Bianchi. Ms. Bird told Moa she was kind of surprised to hear that Ken had found employment in the security business.

—Why's that? he asked.

—Well, said Susan, he just didn't strike me as that type—I thought he was real shady, actually. He actually said that I had a great figure and should consider working as a prostitute. He offered to be my pimp.

Susan was also puzzled, and worried, by Bianchi's colorful proposal because she knew Bianchi had applied for a job with the Bellingham Police department.

Moa at first thought Susan was making this story up, so Susan gave them the name of another woman, Angie Kinneberg, who could further enlighten them as to Bianchi's character.

Angie told Moa that she thought Bianchi was real nice at first. He'd visited her and her girlfriend after Christmas and helped them take down their Christmas tree. But after a while she started to feel something was off. She later found out he was running some business photographing lesbian models for clients down in Los Angeles.

—He's a kinky bastard. He's got a wife though. Kelli. They have a little boy. That guy is really weird, you know.

\* \* \*

Randy Moa didn't know what to think. None of this squared at all with what he knew of his employee. He decided to go to the source and called Bianchi at home.

Ken just laughed the whole thing off. He didn't know about any housesitting job at the Catlow's, and he'd never met anyone called Karen Mandic or Diane Wilder. Besides, he said, that night he was at a sheriff's reserve first-aid meeting.

Bianchi had failed to gain entry with the reserve in Los Angeles, but he had finally met his goal in Bellingham. He had indeed been accepted into the Bellingham Sheriff's Reserve, and the instructor confirmed this when Moa called him.

But Bianchi hadn't been at the first-aid meeting on the night in question. He had never turned up.

Moa called the Bellingham PD and told them Bianchi had lied. He had the stink of culpability on him.

Meanwhile, the security office at Western Washington University had obtained a copy of a key for Karen's apartment. The police went inside to investigate. There, right beside the phone, was a pad with the following note scrawled on top:

*Karen,*
*Please call Ken B.*

*  *  *

The officers found Bianchi at his station at WSA, blithely going about his work. It seemed the phone call from Moa had not rattled him in the slightest. Either that, or he wasn't actually involved in the disappearance of Karen and Diane—but that was now looking impossible.

It was strange. Moa's phone call should have tipped him off that he was in some kind of trouble, and if anything, he should have been on the run by now. Instead, during questioning, the officers found the handsome young security guard utterly polite and cooperative. He was neat, well put together, obviously took pride in his uniform and his appearance. Clean hair and nails, shiny boots. He spoke in a soft voice, and came over relaxed and unconcerned. There seemed no sense of any wrongdoing, or even that he was in any danger from the police. He would, of course, assist the investigation in any way he could.

The atmosphere changed when Bianchi was confronted with the note the officers had found in Karen's apartment. He became indignant, insisting that whoever had really done whatever he was under suspicion for had obviously stolen his identity.

—I would like to know who's been using my name! I'm well known in Bellingham. I was in the newspaper when I left Fred Meyer to come over to WSA in charge of security operations.

Bianchi's haughtiness was delusion, for he had no role as an operations manager at WSA. He was just a guard. Regardless, his self-importance had led him to slip up, because he had now casually disclosed the Fred Meyer connection between himself and Karen, whom he had denied knowing at all.

Still, at this point, the young women were only presumed missing; the police did not have sufficient cause to arrest him, and he was let go.

Detective Mangan, however, was beginning to feel bleakly confident that something bad had happened to the two young ladies. He asked the Highway Patrol to check on sites that might be used to dump bodies or abandon cars, and engaged the news media to describe the missing women and Karen's Mercury Bobcat vehicle to their audience.

Not long after, a woman called the PD about a car that had been abandoned in a wooded area near her home.

The address she gave them was Willow Street, a cul-de-sac leading into forestland not far from the Bayside home of Dr. Catlow. Detectives went to investigate and found Karen Mandic's Mercury Bobcat parked at the end of the road.

The vehicle was locked, but the passenger door was only on the first catch, so officer Robert Knudsen was able to get inside easily. He opened the door, and there in the back seat were Karen and Diane. Their bodies had been tossed in there one on top of the other—like "two sacks of potatoes", he later said.

The two women were found clothed. This was very different to the condition of the bodies discovered in Los Angeles—but the Bellingham PD had no idea about Bianchi's involvement in those murders yet. The subsequent autopsy however revealed that both had been raped, and had been strangled by ligature.

A call was immediately issued for Bianchi's arrest. The police now knew that their suspect was not only armed but dangerous, so they enlisted the assistance of Bianchi's employer, Randy Moa, to entrap him.

Moa wanted to fire Bianchi as of yesterday, but due to the ongoing investigation, he had been playing along. He now radioed Ken in his truck and instructed him to make a security check of a dockland area, where he could be safely cornered.

Down at the dock, the detectives concealed themselves and waited. For a while things were tense. They had to be open to the possibility that Bianchi would never arrive. But Ken simply seemed to have no idea he was in danger. Without a care in the world, he walked straight into the trap.

And suddenly, it was done. It was almost too easy.

Of course, the Bellingham PD had no real concept of just how momentous this arrest was.

# Chapter 20

Bianchi was a practiced killer, but many sloppy errors made in the Washington murders, in combination with the sound detective work of a police unit operating in a small town where information was shared freely, had led to his arrest in less than twenty-four hours. The Bellingham police had managed to accomplish in one day what the Los Angeles detectives had failed to do in a year.

Certain deviations in the Washington murders from the pattern set in Los Angeles represented unwise decisions on the part of the killer—the dumping of bodies fully clothed, the choice to abduct a woman personally know to the perpetrator. Such differences were in fact a signal that Bianchi had been separated from his more practical and restrained Los Angeles sidekick, Angelo Buono. But at this point, the Bellingham officers had no inkling that Bianchi was involved in that string of murders in California that had taken place a year before.

Even so, Bellingham Police Chief Terry Mangan and his men felt sure that it wasn't the first time Bianchi had killed. It was Mangan's contention that despite the mistakes, these murders were too sophisticated to have been the first ones Ken had committed. The errors were of a type consistent with someone not accustomed to operating in a small town. Ken had been caught because in Bellingham, everyone pretty much knew everyone else. Mangan thought if Ken had committed the same crime in a big city, he might well have got away with it. By now, of course, the Bellingham authorities had inspected Bianchi's identification and realized that he had indeed come from Los Angeles—less than a year ago.

Regardless, the arrest of Bianchi in Bellingham in no way guaranteed that he would be connected with the Los Angeles Hillside killings, let alone brought to justice for them.

That this occurred was in part permitted by an accident of fate. Chief Terry Mangan, before joining the police force, had been a Roman Catholic priest and police chaplain. Through his work he had become acquainted with Sister Carmel Marie, who was then the principal of St. Ignatius in Los Angeles, where Delores Cepeda and Sonja Johnson went to school. Sister Marie had introduced Terry to Tony Johnson, who was the bookkeeper for her diocese. Tony Johnson was Sonja Johnson's father.

Tony Johnson hadn't been doing well since his daughter was killed. He blamed himself for his daughter's death, as on the afternoon of Sonja and Delores' disappearance, he had allowed the girls to take the bus home from Eagle Rock Plaza, instead of picking them up in his car. Sadly, despite her best efforts, his wife couldn't help but blame him also. There was much strain on the marriage that ultimately led to separation.

Mangan had been following the Los Angeles murders in the papers since he learned that his friend's daughter had been killed by the Hillside Strangler. Aspects of the Mandic-Wilder murders, in particular the ligature strangulation, made Mangan suspicious of a connection. He thought, at the time, it was a long shot; but the possibility of a link continued to bother him as he and his team set about learning more about Bianchi. The possibility began to look more likely when the Bellingham police saw that Bianchi's driver's license was registered in Los Angeles.

The Bellingham detectives next went to Bianchi's home in Bellingham to conduct a top-to-bottom search. Information found there would further encourage Mangan's suspicions.

Bianchi's common-law wife, Kelli Boyd, seemingly very upstanding, was bewildered and distraught. Her father was a city official and she had always been of the opinion that police were worthy of the utmost admiration and respect. She was forthcoming and helpful with the officers, but Ken had told her he was innocent, and she believed him.

The officers felt a great deal of sympathy for Kelli. They knew that she, unlike Ken, was a Bellingham native; and she struck them just as one of their own. She was a normal young woman trying to raise a family. Her only fault perhaps was that she was not a particularly enquiring person, perhaps too narrowly focused on her own worries and concerns. She and Ken had a baby boy, Ryan, not even a year old. For her to accept that her partner was a rapist and murderer was probably too much to expect.

Kelli, even if she could not believe Ken was a murderer, already had abundant reason to doubt the integrity of his character. It would have been hard for her to have not been aware, for example, of the veritable bonanza of stolen goods stocked in the house.

Police first found a large stash of brand-new tools, still inside their boxes and without price tags. It was later discovered that these had been stolen from the Fred Meyer department store, where Ken had worked before he joined WSA, and where he had become acquainted with Karen Mandic. The detectives also found a mass of brand-new medical supplies. Bianchi had taken these from the Verdugo Hills Hospital in Los Angeles, where he had worked for a time cleaning and delivering medical instruments. Finally, they found a box of brand-new jackets and touch-tone telephones.

It seemed there wasn't anything Ken wouldn't steal, whether he had a use in mind for it or not. What was he going to do with a bunch of telephones?

One of the officers opened a cupboard door in the house and was hammered over the head by a cascade of tinned crabmeat. Bianchi had taken these, clearly with no real plan for what to do with them, from a cold storage company where he was assigned for a job by WSA.

Further items found in the bedroom closet neatly dovetailed with the "character references" of Bianchi supplied by Susan Bird and Angie Kinneberg: professional quality cameras and other photographic equipment. The officers did not yet know about Bianchi's predilection for posing as a cop, but they were nonetheless surprised to also find in the closet a near-mint condition .357 caliber highway patrolman's revolver, complete with its original holster.

So far the Bellingham police only had solid proof of one thing, which was that Bianchi was a thief. This was useful insofar as they now had a good reason to keep him detained while they looked for evidence linking him to the murders of Karen and Diane. But other evidence and items uncovered at his home were pointing in the direction of his complicity in murder also.

In the bedroom, the officers found a pair of uniform trousers with the crotch ripped out. Kelli confirmed that Ken had come home wearing the trousers the evening of the murders. She had found the torn crotch "comical", but added—somewhat poignantly—that she had long ago given up on asking Ken what he got up to when he left the house.

Kelli reported that Ken had come home late that evening, around half past ten, and that he had been sweating profusely, which she thought strange.

Underneath the ripped trousers, they found a work shirt. The fibers in the shirt would later be matched to identical ones found at the Bayside house. The police also found a pair of cowboy boots, the tread of which would be matched to a wet footprint found in Dr. Catlow's kitchen.

Earlier, Detective Knudsen had examined Karen's Mercury Bobcat. Underneath the car, he found a scrape on the gasoline tank. At Dr. Catlow's residence, there was a rock with paint on it that matched the tank. They now knew that Karen's car had at some point been at the Bayside house.

Next, the officers searched Bianchi's VW Beetle and work truck. In the VW, on the floor of the front passenger side, they found a leather briefcase. Inside was a collection of documents relating to a psychiatric counseling service in Los Angeles offered by a "Dr. Ken Bianchi."

The officers now suspected they were dealing with not only a thief, rapist and serial murderer but a practiced con artist.

This impression solidified when a further search of Karen's apartment yielded a fake security business card in which Bianchi purported to be a "Captain Kenneth A. Bianchi". Clearly this "captaincy" was what he had been referring to when he had earlier told the detectives he was "in charge of operations at WSA". Randy Moa told the officers that no such title had ever been authorized.

If Ken had at least expected to come up with a good alibi, his hopes were again dashed. With Kelli having told the detectives that he was not home that night until ten-thirty, and the earlier hours of the evening unaccounted for, witnesses now came forward with information that placed him both at the likely scene of the crime, and at the dumping site, on the evening of the murders. A neighbor of Dr. Catlow's, Mrs. McNeill, told the detectives she had seen a yellow WSA pick-up truck at the Catlow residence around 9:30pm. A second witness, Raymond Spees, claimed he had also seen a yellow WSA pickup truck that night—speeding out of Willow Street, where Karen's Mercury Bobcat was found with the dead girls inside.

With evidence gathered from the witnesses, the Catlow residence and Karen's car now directly implicating Bianchi in the two murders, Chief Mangan decided to call the authorities in Los Angeles. When he told them that they had arrested a suspect named Kenneth Alessio Bianchi on suspicion of double homicide and rape, he was informed that this name had already come up several times in connection with the Hillside Strangler investigation.

The taskforce wired over the composite drawings of the Hillside suspects their forensic artist had prepared earlier. One of these matched Bianchi exactly.

Bellingham now wired over a copy of Ken's fingerprints. George Herrera, an analyst at the LAPD, immediately noticed a characteristic in the prints—a pattern in one of the fingers. It leapt out at him. He had seen it before; twice in fact. They matched a set of prints from the phone booth at the Hollywood public library, and another from the Tamarind apartments following the murder of Kimberly Martin.

There was now hard physical evidence linking Bianchi not only to the Washington murders, but the Hillside slayings.

Bullseye.

# Chapter 21

In Los Angeles the mood was jubilant. With the fingerprint evidence confirming the connection, they now checked their other records on this Kenneth Bianchi locked up in Whatcom County, and all the pieces of the puzzle fell together.

The officers who had previously interviewed Bianchi in Los Angeles had missed the connections between his residential records and the addresses of the victims. But Salerno, who had been off duty when he received the call from Parker Center headquarters, immediately saw that for once this was a suspect with tangible links to the case history. Bianchi had once lived at 809 East Garfield, the same complex where Kristina Weckler had lived, and across the street from the last woman murdered, Cindy Hudspeth. He had also lived at 1950 Tamarind, where Kimberly Martin was lured to her death.

Salerno and Sargeant Dudley Varney now flew up to Bellingham to see what more they could learn from the detectives there.

The news from Bellingham was that Bianchi, so far, had denied everything: if he had killed any women, he didn't remember doing so. They thought this was entirely predictable behavior from a suspect whose physical links to the crime for which he had been arrested were now confirmed. Complete denial and amnesia was his only out. But in the interim, Kelli Boyd had told the officers that Ken's only real friend in Los Angeles had been his cousin Angelo Buono. Varney and Salerno were now confident that they had a solid lead on the identity of the second Hillside Strangler.

At this time, Bob Grogan was returning from a trip to Greeley, Colorado, where he had been following up another false lead in the connection with the case: a woman there had informed the taskforce that her boyfriend, who she had charged with raping her, had confessed to being the Hillside Strangler. Like the erstwhile confessors, he had proved to be a whacko.

Varney put through a call to his partner on 14 January from Bellingham with the news on the break in the case. At hearing the names of the two cousins, Kenneth Bianchi and Angelo Buono, Grogan was astonished and humbled to realize the German detective, "Dr. Shickelgruber", had been correct in his theory that the suspects were Italian and related. He was gratified however that his speculations about the Glendale connection had been confirmed.

Angelo Buono's house and garage were now placed under surveillance. Additionally, an undercover officer would stealth-stalk Buono whenever he left the premises. The detectives would speak with Angelo soon enough, but in the meantime, after so many mistakes made in the investigation, they wanted to be sure they had solid information on which to base any subsequent interrogation or arrest. Because of Angelo's business activities, the police were fairly confident that he was unlikely to skip town, as long as he didn't sense the heat on him. Questioning of Buono would have to wait until Salerno and Varney returned from Washington with the findings from their probe in Bellingham.

In the meantime, Chief Mangan was drawing some disturbing conclusions about what might have happened had he not acted so quickly when Karen Mandic and Diane Wilder had gone missing. Further searches of Bianchi's residence had yielded a list of women who had agreed to pose nude for photography sessions with him. The detectives spoke to a woman on the list who had agreed to meet with Bianchi at the same Bayside residence on the evening of 18 January, the very day that he was arrested. On that same day, she received a call from Bianchi cancelling their rendezvous. Mangan surmised that at that time, Bianchi may have sensed the detectives were closing in on him and thought it wise to call off the meeting.

The Bellingham detectives later learned that Ken had made contact with another woman on the list, but had not made any definite plans to meet her.

Bianchi had obtained the list at Western Washington University, where Karen Mandic and Diane Wilder were studying. The women had registered for jobs as nude models for art classes.

The young woman who had agreed to meet with Bianchi at the Catlow residence on 18 January remained unconvinced that he was a danger to her, even after he had been arrested on suspicion of the Mandic-Wilder murders. She told Terry Mangan that Bianchi was a nice, sincere guy. It was obvious to her that they had arrested the wrong man. She would not be persuaded that she had been his intended victim number three in Washington.

Bianchi himself presented an enigma for the Bellingham cops. Not only did he staunchly deny any involvement in the murders, he claimed he could not remember anything from the times when they had occurred. And he just didn't look or act like a crim. Hell, the guy was a wimp. There was something squirmy and servile, almost feminine about him. The hands that tightened the ligatures around so many necks were not large and powerful, but slender, hairless and white, like the hands of a pianist or a painter. His voice was gentle, a little high in pitch. Kelli had given them the impression he was very conscious of his impression; he fussed over his clothes and hair, like a girl. He wanted the approval of others, especially superiors. In his interactions with the police he was always unfailingly polite, even deferential.

The detectives, who were old hands at dealing with sociopaths and criminals, found Bianchi's continued denials and reports of amnesia unsurprising. Others, such as a social worker brought in to talk with him, were not so sure. It wasn't simply that Bianchi was denying any involvement. If he was purely a con artist, he was so very good at it that he presented an impression of being a complete stranger even to himself. As the evidence mounted against him, Ken continued to appear the all-American boy next door, genuinely horrified by the allegations against him. It was almost as if those atrocities had been the work of a different man entirely.

Eventually, when confronted with irrefutable facts of his guilt, he simply collapsed in tears. Despair and helplessness overwhelmed him, robbed him of all his energies.

He was desperate, he was powerless. He could never have done these things they were accusing him of. Why did they keep insisting that he did?

# Chapter 22

Kelli Boyd was getting nervous. She believed Ken's persistent denials, but she knew he was in serious legal trouble, and had taken the step of scraping together some money to hire an attorney, Dean Brett.

Now she learned that some detectives from Los Angeles were flying to Bellingham to talk with her about Ken. If the thought that Ken had been involved in the murders of Karen Mandic and Diane Wilder wasn't bad enough, now she was being asked to consider the possibility that her husband was the Hillside Strangler.

Frank Salerno and Dudley Varney, together with Bellingham detective Dave McNeal, interviewed Kelli on 14 January 1979.

The officers were not quite sure what to expect. Their feeling based on what they knew of Kelli so far was that she was an innocent victim who knew nothing about Ken's double-life; in effect, knew very little about her husband at all. But of course, they had to be open to the possibility of surprises.

Kelli was only about five-foot-one, slightly plump, blonde, conservatively dressed in a high-necked blouse. Neither plain nor extraordinarily attractive, but very pretty. She seemed vulnerable to the officers and they decided to start with some easy questions to get her comfortable.

They began by asking some general questions about her relationship with Ken. Where did they meet? How long had they been together?

—I met him at my work, at the California Land Title Company. Ken initially worked at a different office, where my sister Linda worked. I went over there for training, and I met him there and I just thought he was a real nice guy. He helped fix my sister's car ... and that's mainly how we got acquainted, and later he was transferred to the main office, and then I was seeing him everyday ...

The California Land Title Company was a real estate office in University City, Los Angeles. Salerno noted a connection with the Hillside case already. Yolanda Washington had applied for a job there. Universal City was also near the Hollywood area.

The detectives learned that Kelli's relationship with Ken had been bumpy. They had met at the real estate company in 1976, not too long after Ken had moved to Los Angeles from Rochester. By May 1977, Kelli was pregnant, and she had moved in with Ken to his apartment at 1950 Tamarind. But problems in their relationship had prompted her to assert her independence, and she had moved out again. Their relationship was on-again, off-again. Ken was bad with money and was unable to hold a steady job. He had been fired from the California Land Title Company when the management found some marijuana in his desk drawer.

She had hoped, she said, that fatherhood would make Ken more responsible, but her wishes never materialized. Eventually she gave up on him and moved back to Bellingham, where she had grown up, to be close to her parents.

But by May 1978 Ken had convinced her to give him another chance. He relocated to Bellingham and they tried to start over. Kelli was encouraged by the fact that Ken had secured a position with WSA, and she praised him as a father to the little boy, but on a personal and intimate level she felt that, if anything, they were more distant than ever.

Salerno quietly nodded to himself, satisfied that the mystery of what the hell Kenneth Bianchi was doing living in Bellingham had been at least partly resolved. He had followed a woman. But he was sure that there had been much more to the story than that.

—What was Ken like? he asked her. How would you describe his character? Was he ever violent?

—Oh, no, said Kelli. He's kind and gentle. He can be the sweetest man. You should see how he dotes on Ryan ...

Kelli as much as told the officers she didn't believe he had killed any girls, in Bellingham or in Los Angeles. That just wasn't him.

—The Ken that I knew could never have hurt or killed anybody.

Even so, her brow furrowed, her eyes clouded slightly, when they talked about real details, times, places and things. There was stuff she just couldn't explain away.

The detectives showed Kelli a photograph of a used dark blue Cadillac that had once been owned by Ken, but which had been repossessed when he could no longer make the payments. On the windshield of the car there was a Los Angeles County seal, the type which identified police vehicles. Kelli nodded somberly, then told the officers that Ken had also had a police badge, just like the men who lived at the Corona Drive house had said.

Ken had, over the years, bequeathed to Kelli a large amount of jewelry. She had to admit there was a good chance much of it was stolen, given Ken's perpetually iffy finances.

When the Bellingham detectives had first searched the couple's home, they found a large collection of jewelry on the dresser, including a gold rams-horn pendant necklace, and a turquoise ring. Nobody knew it yet, but the necklace had belonged to Kimberly Martin, and the ring had come from Yolanda Washington. Ken had been gifting souvenirs from his victims to his wife.

* * *

When asked about Angelo Buono, Kelli made her opinion plain. She did not like Angelo, did not think he was trustworthy or decent, and even seemed to blame him for a share of the problems between Ken and herself.

Ken had frequently goofed off work to go and play cards at Angelo's house, leading him to get fired. Still, Angelo had helped Ken out financially on a few occasions. When Ken and Kelli were broke, Ken might say, "Hey, Angelo owes me some money," and he would go over to Angelo's house and return with twenty or forty dollars.

These handfuls of cash Ken would bring home weren't any result of Angelo's largesse. Back in Los Angeles, further information was about to come to light concerning the nature of the relationship between Ken and Angelo.

After Ken's fingerprints were matched with those from the payphone and the Tamarind Apartments, Bianchi had been publicly named in the media as a suspect in the Hillside murders. Following this, a Bel-Air resident and lawyer named David Wood contacted television reporter Wayne Satz of KABC with information about Bianchi, whose name he had recognized from the news report.

Wood told Satz that one night he had ordered a prostitute for the evening from an outcall service called Foxy Ladies. This young lady had told him that she and another girl were being held as hostage sex slaves by Bianchi and

Buono. Both girls had been regularly beaten and raped by the pair in between servicing hundreds of clients for no pay.

Satz put Wood into contact with the LAPD. Wood told the cops that the name of the girl he had seen was Rebekah Spears. She had been in fear for her life, and he had helped her escape Bianchi and Buono by putting her on a plane to Phoenix. He believed they would be able to track her down there.

Buono was a real charmer, Wood said sarcastically. He'd been infuriated at the theft of his "property" and launched a campaign of harassment against Wood, which did not end until Wood sent his own underworld goon over to Angelo's trim shop to make a point.

Frank Salerno managed to locate Becky Spears, and she told him that the other girl was named Sabra Hannan. Sabra had also returned to Arizona after escaping her ordeal in Los Angeles.

Salerno was able to bring both Becky and Sabra out to Los Angeles from Phoenix for questioning. The Los Angeles detectives now learned that Ken and Angelo had been running a pimping racket in Los Angeles during 1976 and 1977.

With this useful information now in hand, the Los Angeles detective team decided to seek out Angelo for interrogation.

Detectives Bob Grogan and Pete Finnegan had already visited Buono twice for short preliminary interviews in late January and early February; these sessions were simply designed to get a sense of how cooperative he was likely to be.

The answer so far was "not very". Buono had acted as though he was happy to help the police, but had then proceeded to lie about just about everything. He had said he didn't really know his cousin Kenny. He'd been acquainted with him while he was living in Los Angeles, but he distanced himself, characterizing Ken as being largely "a mystery" to him.

The detectives had done enough homework on Angelo to know this was very likely untrue. Despite forty-two-year-old Buono's outward appearance as a respected local businessman, the officers learned that he already had a colorful criminal history and plenty of associates who could testify to his rapacious sexual appetite and perversions, and his propensity for sexual violence. All of this fit with the statements given by David Wood, Becky Spears and Sabrah Hannan implicating Angelo with Ken in sexual slavery and rape.

So far, they had this to work with.

## A City Owned

\* \* \*

Angelo, like his cousin Ken, originally hailed from Rochester, New York. Born to first generation Italian-American emigrants from the town of San Buono, Italy, on 5 October 1934, Angelo had moved to Los Angeles with his mother Jenny and his sister Cecilia at five years of age after his parents divorced.

Jenny's sister, Frances Scioliono Bianchi, was Ken's mother, but not his biological mother. Like many serial killers, Ken was adopted. He lived in Rochester with his mother and did not follow Angelo to Los Angeles until 1976. In that sense, Angelo had not lied to the cops. The two were not as close as you might expect full-blooded cousins to be.

In the early years, Buono was nominally a Catholic, but never bothered to attend church. He was also a lousy student and was forever skipping school, knowing that Jenny, who had a full-time job, would be unable to control his activities. By the age of 14, Buono was bragging about raping and sodomizing young local girls, and it's likely that this is how he spent the time he should have otherwise been devoting to his studies.

Despite having lived in sunny, hip California since he was five, Angelo was like a slice of the old world planted in the new. He staunchly maintained his Italian traditions, perpetually flying the national flag at half-mast from his lawn, and keeping his large and comfortable, but rather sparsely furnished, home immaculately clean.

In a quirk of character deviating from his otherwise resolute stance of masculine entitlement, neat-freak Buono liked to do his cleaning himself, and was forever pacing back and forth with the duster. A lover of animals, he had a dog called Sparky, pet rabbits and a carefully maintained tropical aquarium.

As much as Angelo loved his pets, he loathed women. From an early age he had been given to calling his mother Jenny "cunt" and "whore". This troubled relationship became the template for all his future relations with women, whom Buono unilaterally referred to as "cunts", without a hint of apology.

As much as Angelo hated the "cunts," he couldn't get enough of them either, and his life was romantically and sexually complicated, to say the least. By the time Ken was arrested in Washington, Buono had married three times, and had fathered eight children, some of whom for which he had received convictions for failure to pay child support. He had received additional convictions for car theft, assault and rape, and had spent much time in and out of juvie and prison. His wives, who were at first attracted to his macho style, would quickly discover his entrenched hatred for women. He had an outrageous appetite for sex and the more degrading and painful it was for the women, the more he enjoyed it. Inflicting pain only added to his sexual pleasure and there were times that he was so abusive, many of the women feared for their lives.

Despite this unsavory profile, Buono was well known and respected around Glendale and Hollywood for his auto upholstering work. High-school dropout Buono had really found his feet when he set up his business at forty. Angelo was a skilled craftsman with a reputation as a fair businessman. His services were highly sought.

Everyone knew that a man without a good-looking car in Los Angeles was hardly a man at all. Many high-profile types went to Angelo to make sure their car looked as good inside as it did outside. The big swinging dicks of Hollywood, guys like Frank Sinatra, were his best customers.

Despite Angelo's criminal history of rape and assault, the detectives learned during their research that not all or even most of the women who had sex with Angelo did so against their will. Buono had a reputation as the local lothario, and was perpetually surrounded by a bevy of young women vying for his attentions.

This Don Juan was known by a couple of monikers within his circle: the "Italian Stallion" and "The Buzzard". Somehow, Angelo pulled off sleazy stereotypes such as owning a waterbed, and refusing to wear anything other than red silk underwear, with a certain elan.

Grogan and Finnegan were puzzled and rather disgusted by Angelo's success with women, because the man they met at Colorado Street during those preliminary interviews in February 1979 could in no way be described as attractive.

He was rather short, slight of frame, with a mass of curly dyed black hair, a large crooked nose and equally crooked teeth. His skin was like greased leather and he spoke in a guttural, lisping voice that summoned to mind the snake and the reptile. Grogan remarked to Finnegan that he didn't think he had ever seen a man who more closely resembled a lump of excrement.

Grogan was even more appalled when he learned that his own girlfriend, her curiosity piqued after hearing Grogan's descriptions of Angelo as "slimy" and "ugly", and of his reputation as a ladies man, had gone to Angelo's shop to check him out personally.

Grogan's girlfriend thought that while Buono was not conventionally attractive, there sure was something magnetic about him.

—If I didn't know who he was, she said, I might have dropped my clothes right there!

—Goddammit! yelled Grogan. Don't you ever go anywhere near that guy again!

* * *

Detectives Grogan and Finnegan interviewed Angelo at the trim shop on the afternoon of February 6, in the office attached to Angelo's garage. The session was recorded on an audio device Grogan had brought concealed in his jacket.

The men arrived unannounced in the late afternoon when they thought Buono would be finishing up for the day. Angelo seemed unruffled by their appearance; he was neither welcoming nor hostile. This made it appear that he had nothing to hide, but was probably a better indicator of his absolute confidence in his ability to stonewall the police and provide zero information of value.

As the men sat down to talk they were briefly interrupted by a loud buzzing noise.

—My wife, Angelo said casually. She must be heading out.

This was a surprise: it appeared he had recently married again, for the fourth time.

The bride, they learned, was a young Chinese immigrant named Tai-Fun Fanny Leung. Angelo's buzzer went off whenever she was coming or going from the house, so he knew where she was even when he couldn't leave the garage. Buono might deny that he knew much about Ken or the Hillside murders, but obviously he took a lordly attitude with the women in his life, and it all solidified a certain consistent impression of character.

Grogan asked Angelo if he had ever been to the Robin Hood Inn, a local Glendale watering hole where the detectives had learned from a waitress that Angelo had been seen speaking to Cindy Hudspeth, who had at one time been a part-time server there.

Angelo not only denied ever having been to the Robin Hood, he stated—rather unconvincingly, given its location right on Glendale Avenue—that he didn't even know where it was.

—I don't drink no booze, he said proudly.

The officers later learned that he had been telling the truth about that at least. In most people abstaining from alcohol might be considered a mark of restraint and maturity. In Angelo's case they thought it likely he had never developed a taste for liquor because of the loss of control it might cause. Angelo would want to have his wits about him at all times. He would never yield an advantage to anyone.

Next, Grogan asked Angelo about Becky Spears and Sabra Hannan. Did he know either of those girls? He pulled out two photos and showed them to Angelo.

Angelo said he'd never heard of Becky Spears before, but he knew Sabra through Ken. They had a "thing" going at one time, he explained.

—What? They were dating? Sleeping together?

—I dunno, man. I ain't getting in Ken's business.

So Angelo didn't really know Ken, but he knew that Ken had a "thing" with Sabra. Interesting.

What about the Foxy Ladies outcall service? Had he had any dealings with them?

Angelo admitting knowing the owner and the driver, but apparently couldn't identify the driver from a picture. He explained vaguely that he met them "through another guy." Their suspect was pretending to be cooperative, but he wasn't giving anything away.

Finally Grogan lost patience.

—Hey Angelo, let's stop wasting time. We've already talked to Becky, we've already talked to Sabra. We already talked to David Wood, the lawyer from Bel-Air you tried to screw over. You and Ken were running broads!

Angelo rolled his eyes.

—I ain't never been running no broads. Look man, I'm just a regular guy, like you. I got a job to do. You got a job to do. So let's get it over with and let each other do their job.

Angelo was calm and confident. He continued with his strategy, which would remain much the same henceforward: denying any knowledge or involvement in anything, and where he did know or admit something, pinning it all on Kenny.

—Those girls, he said, that Becky and Sabra... they were working for Kenny I think. I had nothing to do with it.

Buono now invented a ludicrous tale that Becky and Sabra had set themselves up as prostitutes and were running their operation from his house, with Kenny acting as pimp, but he was never a part of it. He admitted to having had sex with the two girls, but it was all consensual—they wanted it, of course—and he had no idea how old they were.

Now Grogan was really angry. He decided to get right to the point. He got into Angelo's face and started yelling:

—Me and my partner here, we work homicide, right? So we don't care about pimping or prostitution unless it relates to the question we're asking. We already got plenty on you, scumbag. Not just about the beating and the rapes. We got a witness saw you pick up Judy Miller on Sunset. We got another one seen you abducting Lauren Wagner with Kenny. See where this is going?!

To prove he meant business, Grogan removed the audio recorder from his jacket and placed it in front of them on the desk. For a moment, Angelo looked worried, his eyes shifting uneasily to the floor. Grogan thought he was about to break him. But just as quickly, Angelo regained his composure.

—I didn't do no murders. I ain't abducted nobody. You're hassling the wrong guy.

Angelo was so complacent, he waived his right to have an attorney present.

The detectives realized they probably still weren't going to get anything much out of him, but they started their interrogation anew. To their surprise, this time things went a little better.

The officers now got Buono to admit that his cousin Ken was rather more than just a casual acquaintance: actually, Angelo knew Ken quite well. Ken had lived with him on Colorado Street for a time after he first arrived in Los Angeles from Rochester. Angelo also told the detectives that Ken had later lived at 809 East Garfield and 1950 Tamarind for periods of time. He mentioned meeting "that fat bitch" Kelli Boyd on a few occasions when he visited Ken at the Tamarind apartments. He also confirmed that Ken had worked for the California Land Title Company, had applied to the LAPD Reserves, and participated in the ride-along program.

The information Buono supplied did not implicate himself directly, but it certainly was building the case against Ken, and tying him to Ken in important places and periods of time.

The detectives wanted to know if Buono, like Bianchi, had any cop paraphernalia. Angelo said he had never owned a police badge, real or fake. He pointed the finger at Bianchi again, mentioning both a county seal on the window of Ken's dark blue Cadillac and "some kind" of badge. Angelo, however, always clouded his admissions in vague terms or even in a convenient imprecision borne of his own semi-literacy. It seemed that, for whatever reason, he wasn't entirely comfortable with ratting out Ken.

—He had something like that, Angelo said of the badge, but I'm not sure. You could buy stuff like that down at the swap meet. They got everything down there. Man, you can get fake badges all over town. Lotsa guys got those things.

That was true, and the detectives knew it. It was part of what made their job difficult. The fact that a guy had a fake police badge didn't make him the Hillside Strangler.

They already knew that Ken had a county seal on his Cadillac, the one that had been repossessed when he failed to make the payments. But Buono's confirmation of the fact was potentially useful. A short while ago Angelo had been denying he knew anything about Ken at all. But now he had admitted he was aware of the very facts that tied Ken to the case. He was a short step from implicating himself.

Next, Buono offered some enlightenment as to the fake psychology credentials the Bellingham police had found in the attaché case in Ken's car. There was an office he was sharing with some guy out at North Hollywood, he said. Ken had these things hanging on the wall, certificates and stuff.

The office Buono referred to was located in the building in Lankershim where Jan Sims had her eerie encounter with Ken Bianchi in the parking lot when she was waiting for her daughter. The detectives now had a sense that Ken had been posing as a psychiatrist or psychologist and receiving payment for services from clients on the basis of bogus credentials.

Grogan probed Angelo's knowledge of a list of locations tied to the Hillside murders, either as dumping or abduction sites: Forest Lawn Drive, Angeles Crest, the Eagle Rock Plaza, La Crescenta. Angelo denied he had been to any of these places with Ken, but he said he knew all of those places either as part of driving routes he took around the city, or because he had visited them with friends or family.

Grogan showed Angelo photos of each of the Hillside victims. Did he know any of these girls? Had he seen any of them before?

Buono's voice was a monotone as he stated either having never seen the girl before or "maybe" having seen one or other of them on TV. He never flinched and seemed bored, even indifferent. What the girls had suffered clearly didn't bother him, even if he hadn't had anything to do with their deaths.

Finally, Grogan asked Angelo point blank if he was involved in the murders. Angelo gave the answer that he would stick with for as long as possible: any knowledge he had was from the media.

If everything he knew came from the media, that implied he had been following the case in the news. Had he formed any views about who the Hillside Strangler was?

Buono continued to hide behind his own apparent ignorance.

—I don't read, so I didn't see nuthin' in the papers. I might have seen the odd thing on television.

Next he made a transparent and risible effort to throw the detectives off the trail.

—A friend of mine bought the subject up once, and I said, maybe they should be looking for two girls who done it or maybe a guy and a girl. Because, you know, a girl would jump quicker into a car when there was a woman in the car, than if there were two dudes.

Lastly, the detectives asked Angelo if he had any contact with Ken since he moved to Bellingham.

No, Angelo said firmly. For once they thought he might be telling the truth.

Grogan and Finnegan suspected there had been a "break up" between Angelo and Ken. Kelli Boyd had not been the only attraction for Ken in Bellingham. Something had gone down between Ken and Angelo in Los Angeles, Ken had made a break for it, and now there was no love lost. But the only allusion Angelo made to any conflict between them was Ken's propensity to borrow money without repaying it.

—Look, he was a real nice guy, Angelo said, he'd give you the shirt off his back. But sometimes he wants something and you don't give it to him, he gets mad. And I figure, you know, why get in a hassle for a few dollars. I'd rather forget about it. Then don't loan him the money next time, see?

So Ken had a temper. Did he think Ken might have been involved in the murders?

—Could be, Buono said thoughtfully. You never know. He was a little crazy. He coulda lost his mind.

\* \* \*

The detectives learned more about Angelo from his former wife, Candy. She was hardly willing to vouch for his integrity. She told them that Angelo had routinely assaulted her both physically and sexually; intriguingly, it was his want to tie her to the bed by the wrists and the ankles prior to violently raping and sodomizing her.

Grogan tried to feel out the possibility of getting Buono's children to talk to the police.

No way, she said. Buono's kids were all terrified of him. Her son Peter was convinced Angelo was going to kill him, and in her opinion, Angelo would not hesitate to destroy anyone who crossed him or went behind his back.

One interesting and important piece of information Candy passed on concerned the hillside trash heap at Landa Street, where the bodies of Dollie Cepeda and Sonja Johnson had been found. This area was very well known to Buono. He had always colloquially referred to it as the "cow patch," and had taken her and the children there for family picnics, of all things.

Another geographic connection to the case surfaced when they learned that a former girlfriend of Angelo's, Melinda Hooper, lived on Alta Terrace Drive, where Judy Miller's body had been dumped. Hooper's residence, a big two-story white house she shared with her parents, was actually more or less right next to the dump location, at number 2844.

Angelo's old flat mate, Hollywood actor Artie Ford, also had some interesting information for the police. Artie said he never got into Angelo's business, but that Angelo had some "peculiarities" and had made a few off-hand remarks that reminded him to stay well out.

Artie said Buono had boasted of raping one of his stepdaughters, Annette, citing the fact that at only fourteen years of age she "needed to be broken in"; when he himself finished with Annette, he passed her to his sons for their own sexual use. Buono's son Peter had claimed at one time that Angelo had sodomized him too.

The house that Artie shared with Angelo was near a high school. One day, Artie had stumbled upon Buono masturbating while admiring the school children through binoculars.

Then there was the time Buono was angry with Candy after they had a fight. He decided to sneak into her house and leave the gas on in the kitchen, hoping she would light a cigarette and blow herself and the house to smithereens.

—My God, Artie had said, what about the children?

—Fuck the children, Angelo said.

As if all of this was not enough to raise suspicion of his involvement in the brutal rape and murder of ten women in Los Angeles, there was the fact that Buono's teen idol was known to be the so-called "Red Light Bandit", Caryl Chessman.

Chessman was a robber and rapist who was responsible for a string of attacks in and around Los Angeles in the 1940s. Chessman lured his victims by following them in their cars to secluded areas. Posing as a police officer, he would shine a torch light through the windows and ask them to exit the vehicle, whereupon he would rob and, in the case of females, rape them.

# Chapter 23

In Washington, the Bellingham detectives were hard at work firming up the case against Ken in the slayings of Karen Mandic and Diane Wilder.

In the weeks following Ken's arrest, officers Fred Nolte and Robert Knudsen returned to the Bayside residence of Dr. Catlow and swept the entire house for physical evidence. From this exercise a picture of exactly how Karen and Diane had met their deaths was emerging. Nolte and Knudsen deduced that the exact murder location was a set of stairs leading down into the basement.

The detectives began at the bottom of the stairwell and worked their way up, combing the steps on hands and knees with a torch and tweezers. On the sixth step they found a pubic hair. On the ninth and tenth steps they found long blonde and dark hairs. These hairs were later identified as having come from Karen and Diane respectively. The pubic hair was matched to Bianchi. With that, they were ready to go to court.

On 26 January 1979, Kenneth Bianchi was charged with first-degree murder in the deaths of Karen Mandic and Diane Wilder in the Whatcom County Superior Court. Prosecuting attorney David McEachran requested Bianchi be held without bail following his arraignment on the murder charges. At McEachran's request, Judge Jack Kurtz sealed affidavits filed by the prosecution containing specifics of the charges and probable cause. A gag order was also placed on the proceedings at the request of defense attorney Dean Brett.

Ken, despite everyone's advice to the contrary, continued to insist somebody else must have killed Karen and Diane. He just wasn't capable of such a thing. The evidence was irrefutable, but Bianchi didn't care: he would never admit to doing something he knew he didn't do, even if that meant his own death.

And that was exactly what it meant: having pled innocent on both counts, Judge Kurtz of the Whatcom County Superior Court set a trial date of 8 March. Kenneth Bianchi was now facing the death penalty in Washington State.

* * *

Today, Dean Brett is an accomplished attorney for Whatcom County specializing in personal injury and wrongful death. Back in the late seventies, he was only recently out of law school, and had taken a few criminal cases due to the lack of a public defender system at the time in Bellingham. In consideration of Kelli's financial situation and his own workload he had agreed to take Ken's case on the basis that he would work only on weekends for a small retainer fee. With little time and meager resources, Dean Brett was trying to put Ken Bianchi's defense together. The difficulty of his task was compounded by Bianchi's apparent inability to remember anything about the night of the murders.

When first questioned by Brett, Ken claimed he had been "driving around" that evening, some distance from the Bayside house. When Brett reminded Bianchi of the incontrovertible evidence placing him at the Bayside residence at the time in question, Ken then stated that he had invented the story about driving around in order to fill the gap in his memory for the period of time concerned.

Brett was one of those who Bianchi left scratching his head. He found it impossible to square the softly spoken, deferential Bianchi with the exceedingly violent nature of the criminal charges against him.

He was of a more liberal turn of mind than most Whatcom attorneys, and was definitely one who subscribed to the view "innocent until proven guilty". But he was in no way gullible or easily swayed.

The cynical and frequently correct view is that a defense attorney does whatever he does, and marshals all opinion and evidence, merely with a view to exonerating his client. Such claims were made about Dean Brett. However Brett himself insists that when Bianchi told him he was innocent, he began to believe him—at least in the sense that he believed Bianchi did not remember killing anybody.

Brett was also concerned about his client's frame of mind in general. To Brett, Ken seemed confused and distraught to the point of being suicidal; indeed, his client threatened he might end his own life should he have the means.

Bianchi was horrified by the possibility that he might have been responsible for the murders of the two young ladies. All the evidence was pointing at him, and yet he had no memory of the events, and didn't think himself even remotely capable of such an act.

Brett decided to call on John Johnson, a psychiatric social worker who had formerly worked at the University of Montana. Johnson spent several sessions with Ken during February 1979, trying both to calm the young defendant and get beneath his defenses.

Ken seemed enveloped in a kind of catatonic numbness. At times, sobs of despair would break through. He seemed most concerned about his family. He was sick with worry about Kelli and Ryan. How would they cope without him? And he was preoccupied with how his mother would be dealing with all this. At her age she didn't need all this stress. It would make her sick.

He had taken great pride in his work at WSA. Things had seemed to be on the upswing for him in Bellingham, and now this. During the sessions Ken, nominally a Roman Catholic, anxiously fumbled a set of rosary beads.

—I have drifted from my faith, he said. But at a time like this Christ is all I have. I pray daily. What else can I do?

Like Brett, Johnson found it impossible to reconcile the seemingly intelligent, sensitive personality he saw before him with that of a rapist and murderer. He began to suspect that Bianchi's amnesia had something to do with the conundrum. Johnson reported this possibility back to Brett, and hinted at it to Bianchi.

In the meantime, in order to come to grips with this most peculiar case, and amidst the dearth of useful information coming from his client, Brett had begun calling anybody and everybody who had known Bianchi in the past, and digging up any records on him that he could find from Los Angeles and Rochester, New York, where Ken had been born and raised.

A bizarre and fascinating picture was emerging, one that suggested a different direction for the defense. He decided he needed the assistance of a psychiatric expert to figure it all out, so at Johnson's suggestion, Brett next telephoned Donald T. Lunde of Stamford University, America's first forensic psychiatrist, and asked him to come to Bellingham and examine Bianchi.

During this conversation, Lunde asked Brett whether he thought Bianchi had killed the two co-eds in Washington.

—Yeah, he did it, said Brett. But I don't have the foggiest idea why. I'm no doctor, but ... I suspect this guy has some kind of serious mental problem.

Brett had established, by means of records located in Rochester, that Ken had a prior history of consultation with psychiatrists in childhood. He forwarded copies of these records to Lunde so he could prepare for his session with Bianchi.

The records documented an early history of psychological and possible physical abuse at the hands of Ken's adoptive mother, Frances, as well as petit-mal seizures, and fits of trancelike daydreaming in which Ken's eyes would roll back, and he would rock back and forward or turn his head from side to side. Lunde was particularly interested in the description of the child's "trances" and an accompanying notation provided by the assessing doctor: "he appears to not know what is going on".

If Ken lost awareness of his surroundings during these episodes, Lunde wondered if they were a possible forerunner to an amnesic or dissociative condition he suffered in the present.

By this time, with Bianchi still flatly denying any involvement in, or memory of, the murders of Karen Mandic and Diane Wilder, and the possibility that Ken Bianchi was insane looming as a possibility, Dean Brett was urging Bianchi to change his plea.

The Supreme Court case of *North Carolina v Alford* in 1970 had established a precedent for the so-called Alford plea, in which it was affirmed that there are no constitutional barriers to prevent a judge accepting a guilty plea from a defendant even where the defendant protests his innocence. A guilty plea to save Ken's life. Then again, if Ken was insane, he was not competent to stand trial.

Judge Kurtz offered Brett the opportunity for the defense to alter its plea, with a time limit of thirty days. Dean Brett needed to know whether Kenneth Bianchi was mentally competent to plead or stand trial.

\* \* \*

Lunde interviewed Ken Bianchi at the Whatcom county jail on 10 March. The defendant was neat and clean shaven, but pale and very thin. He said he had been eating little; he had no appetite. He clutched at the rosary and turned it over and over in his hands as he talked.

Lunde's first task in the interview, as he saw it, was to try and get Bianchi to open up about some of the history they had identified in the medical and psychiatric reports from Rochester. By any measure he should have been a very troubled man, but that was not what they were seeing. Ken was as nice as pie, apparently just a regular fellow who had ended up in a horrible jam, with no idea how or why.

After some preliminary questions Lunde got right down to it.

—How would you describe your mother, Ken?

Bianchi's face lit up and he smiled at the mention of Frances.

—She was a real saint. You know, the kind of woman who would do anything for anybody. I've got all the respect in the world for my mother.

Ken went on and on, waxing lyrical about Saint Frances. She was the kindest, most loving mother a boy could have.

Lunde furrowed his brow, referring back to his notes. Something was definitely amiss here. Ken had in fact almost been taken away from Frances several times by social services on suspicion of child abuse. How could it be that Ken's denial of his history was so entrenched? Was this denial the same source as that which his lack of memory of the murders sprang?

Dr. Lunde, focusing on the problems presented by Ken's pattern of denial and amnesia, suggested to Dean Brett that sodium amytal be administered to Ken to unlock his memory. Sodium amytal was known colloquially known as "truth serum" in the 1950s and 1960s, when it was used by US and Soviet intelligence during the Cold War. The chemical had been shown to assist people to recall things otherwise blocked from their memory.

There were several problems with this idea, however. Dean Brett was working to the prosecution's deadline, and Lunde could not return again to Bellingham to supervise and record the procedure. Additionally, sodium amytal, which is similar in effect to a major anesthetic, is best administered in a hospital, and the authorities would not allow Ken to leave the prison—even if a local hospital had been willing to take him.

As a compromise, it was decided to try hypnosis instead of the sodium amytal to open up Ken's mind.

Lunde wasn't entirely on board with the suggestion, and warned Brett that hypnosis was vulnerable to abuse and malingering in a way that sodium amytal was not. A competent prosecutor could persuade most juries to dismiss the resulting evidence.

Despite his misgivings, Lunde suggested Brett might get in touch with Dr. John G. Watkins, an expert in the field of hypnosis and dissociative reaction from the University of Montana.

Together with his wife, Helen Watkins, Dr. Watkins had developed a new therapy known as ego-state therapy, which explored repressed personalities as the cause of psychological problems in clients. This therapy is a psychodynamic approach in which techniques of group and family therapy are employed to resolve conflicts between various "ego states" that constitute a "family of self" within a single individual. The theory held that although covert ego states do not normally become overt except in a true multiple personality, they are hypnotically activated and made accessible for contact and communication with the therapist.

Watkins' credentials were impressive: he was a professor of psychology at the University of Montana and a diplomat of the American Board of Professional Psychology and the American Board of Psychological Hypnosis. Even so, his views on the prevalence of MPD (Multiple Personality Disorder) were controversial.

Where conventional medical and psychiatric opinion held the disorder was rare, Watkins believed MPD was under-diagnosed, and that in cases of amnesia, MPD was often a distinct candidate for an underlying explanatory pathology.

Watkins' curiosity about Ken's case had been stoked not only by Lunde's descriptions of the "patient" as presenting a confounding enigma, but something he learned the cops had found in Ken's basement at the Bellingham home he shared with Kelli: a statue which was apparently a high school art project. The statue had two heads: one a normal, smiling man, the other a grimacing monster.

Was this evidence of Ken's awareness that he had a "split mind"—all the way back in the distant past, well before he was charged with any murder?

# Chapter 24

In Los Angeles, the news that the defense had called in Watkins to examine Bianchi was about as welcome as a cancer diagnosis. Calling in an "expert" such as Watkins could only mean they were working towards an insanity plea.

Salerno tried to be philosophical.

Well, he thought, playing devil's advocate with himself, suppose the guy *is* crazy?

It was true that Kenneth Bianchi was a relative unknown to them. The word from Bellingham was that he had been consistent in protesting his innocence from the beginning, and continued to claim amnesia for the time of the crime for which he was now facing charges.

But any seasoned cop was going to see it for the balderdash it likely was. What were the chances, really? And supposing it was all a sham, twelve women were dead, and the most Bianchi would get was time in a psychiatric institution, meals, board and therapy all paid for until he was declared "sane", and early release. Even worse, any case against Angelo Buono could collapse, as Bianchi would not be able to stand as a witness in those proceedings if deemed legally insane.

With this danger uppermost in his mind, Salerno initiated a request that a delegation from Los Angeles be allowed to attend the sessions between Watkins and Bianchi. Dean Brett consented and the session was scheduled for 21 March.

\* \* \*

Salerno and Detective Pete Finnegan flew to Washington and met together with Dean Brett, John Watkins and John Johnson at the Whatcom county jail to discuss the arrangements. The plan was that Dr. Watkins would conduct the session with Ken, with Johnson in the room operating the recording equipment, but not participating. The session would be recorded on video in its entirety. Salerno and Finnegan would watch from behind a screen in another room. They would be able to see Ken, but Ken would not see them.

Prior to the interview, Ken had been given a copy of the DePaul Clinic report from Rochester, the contents of which had so concerned Dr. Lunde.

By reading the report, Ken had arguably been given the opportunity to tailor his act to the impression the psychiatric experts were forming of his past. The context in which the defense was developing was now clearly one of childhood abuse and subsequent possible mental illness.

On the other hand, the clinic's reports were themselves utterly authentic, and in that sense, a legitimate defense based on Ken's mental state was an entirely plausible outcome.

\* \* \*

Bianchi appeared in his drab prison overalls, his dark hair grown out considerably from the time of his arrest, wavy and slightly unkempt. He was around six feet tall, not exactly powerfully built, but certainly muscular and evenly proportioned. More than capable of ending a life with his bare hands, should he choose to.

He wasn't cuffed or restrained and nobody knew quite what to expect. Ken might at any moment have some kind of dissociative psychotic episode, or if he was just a regular sociopathic criminal with a bad temper, that could end badly for them as well.

Watkins had to approach the situation with all that in mind. He began by making small talk: asking Ken inoffensive questions about how he was feeling, how he had been doing in prison, and what his thoughts had been of late.

Bianchi was subdued but polite. His answers were neither effusive nor curt. He mused aloud with a quality of somber introspection. He appreciated all the trouble everyone was going to. He was going to do everything they asked; the dutiful patient complying cooperatively with the demands of diagnosis and treatment.

The topic of conversation quickly drifted to Frances. Ken said that he had been feeling differently about her since he had read the DePaul Clinic report. It made him aware of his own very great capacity for denial. There was so much in his life and his past he simply chose not to think about.

He began to rattle on in a kind of meandering, circuitous style that all who examined him would over time get very used to. It was trademark Kenneth Bianchi oratory. It said a lot while not saying very much; it might have been deliberately vague, or it might have simply signified a great lack of self-understanding.

—I mean, he said, you could have said anything you wanted to about my mother. You could have talked until you were blue in the face, to say she was a bad mother, to discredit her. And I would have fought tooth and nail, thumbscrew ... I mean I would have argued and disagreed with anything you had to say. Because I always had the greatest love and respect for my mother. But now, I'm starting to wonder ...

—Go on Ken, said Dr. Watkins. What's on your mind?

—I mean, I—I read this report and it raises the question ... I mean I obviously had serious problems, some worse than others, some that could develop into real serious problems down the line. And now I wonder, maybe I should have had more help, more professional help ...

Salerno and Finnegan glanced at each other, eyebrows raised. Already they didn't like the direction this was going. But it was about to get worse.

—Ken, said Dr. Watkins, if you hide from yourself ... if you don't know what you really are ... I'm getting this sense that there's this rosy picture, that you had before. It's a little bit like fooling yourself. Maybe that's been going on for a long time.

Ken nodded. Yes, doctor, that's exactly what it's like.

Watkins warned Ken that he might not like what he learned about himself when he opened the closed doors in his mind. But that was what was necessary for any "healing" to occur.

Ken agreed enthusiastically. Despite any fears he might have, he was willing to explore the truth about himself and his past.

At this, Salerno and Finnegan were shaking their heads, incredulous. To their minds, Watkins' approach and line of questioning was so incredibly leading as to render any result useless. It had already been assumed that Ken had some kind of psychological defect which rendered him amnesic at key times. It was also being taken for granted that Ken was a stranger to himself, that he didn't know what deeds he was capable of, that his conscious self legitimately didn't know or remember anything about the murders.

Salerno was thinking back to the interview with Kelli Boyd. She had never made any mention of witnessing amnesic lapses with Ken.

And just suppose, for argument's sake, that it was true. The guy was a whackjob who, from time to time, blacked out and then turned into a homicidal maniac. That would mean, that back in Los Angeles, this was something that only conveniently happened when he was hanging out with his cousin, Angelo Buono. The rest of the time he was Mr. Normal. How likely was that?

The truth was the detectives and the psychiatric experts were viewing all this very differently. Watkins was viewing Ken as a patient; the detectives were viewing Ken as a serial murder suspect.

Now it was time for Watkins to get down to business: to the meat of what the session was about. He gently explained to Ken that he would be employing hypnosis to get underneath his psychic defenses and "recover his memories".

Everything that happened in his life, and all the associated feelings and responses, had been psychically recorded since his birth, he explained. Ken's conscious mind didn't remember that stuff for his own protection.

—But sometimes, Ken, those defenses become so rigid they don't protect us anymore. They get in the way of our healing. Understand?

Ken nodded.

Ken needn't worry about anything, Watkins said. It was perfectly safe. The hypnotic procedure was purely a matter of inducing a state of deep relaxation, and Ken would not be hurt by what he remembered, at least not during the hypnosis itself.

Watkins began by suggesting Ken relax, and feel in turn each of his limbs, and then his entire body, grow heavy. Enjoy the feeling of not paying attention to things, to ignore everything but the heavy feelings in his body. His legs, heavy like the limbs on the trunk of a tree. Now his arms too, heavier, heavier. His whole body sinking. The world getting warm and heavy.

—Isn't it good just to let go ... to have a deep feeling of calm and peace ... deeper and deeper ...

Ken's eyelids sagged, his arms slackening on their rests. He seemed to be melting into the chair. As far as anyone could tell, Watkin's hypnotic induction was working.

Even so, Salerno and Finnegan were skeptical. Their suspicions and outrage would grow when Watkins now proceeded to the centerpiece of the session, in which he would invite an alter, already presumed to be lurking within Bianchi's mind, to speak:

—I've talked a bit to Ken but I think that maybe there's another part of Ken that I haven't talked to, that maybe feels a bit differently. And I would like that other part to come to talk to me. And when it's here and then the left hand will lift up off the chair to indicate to me that the other part is here that I would like to talk to. Would you please come, Part, so I can talk to you? Part, would you come and lift Ken's hand to indicate to me that you are here?

At first, there was no response. Watkins pleaded and cajoled with "Part", but Part did not come. The doctor decided to try a slightly different tack.

—Part, you don't have to speak with Ken if you don't want to. You can just speak to me. Anything you tell me will be between you and me. I won't share anything with Ken. Part, if you would like to talk to me, I would like to ask you to communicate with me by raising Ken's left hand.

Slowly, without any perceptible effort, Ken's left hand began to lift off the chair rest.

—Yes, said a voice. Deeper than Ken's usual speaking voice.
—Hello?
—I am here.

Watkins brought his thumb to his lips and leaned forward in his chair, obviously thrilled by the transformation.

—Part, he said excitedly, are you the same as Ken or different in some way?
—I'm not Ken. Do I look like Ken?

"Part's" tone was indignant, almost disgusted by the comparison. Whoever was speaking now clearly did not care for Ken.

Now Watkins almost fell over himself trying not to cause any further offense. He wanted "Part" to stick around after all.

—Now just make yourself comfortable in the chair there. Do you have a name? What shall I call you?
—It's Steve. You can call me Steve.

Johnson, holding the camera, stepped back slightly. He had already intuited that this Steve character was not particularly friendly.

—Nice to meet you, Steve. Now we don't have to talk about Ken. It's you I want to know about. Tell me about yourself. What do you do?

## A City Owned

At the mention of Ken, Steve's mood took another dive.
—That fuckin' sap ...
—Who? Ken?
—I hate him. That fuckin' pansy.
—Why do you hate Ken?
—He's such an ass. He puts up with all her shit.
—Who? Who's shit does he put up with?
—My mother. I hate my mother. I hate a lot of people.
—So Ken's mother is your mother?
—Not exactly. Well she is in a way ...

Watkins was listening intently, eagerly soaking up each new revelation. He stroked his facial fuzz like a scientist observing a test tube bubbling over. What would come next?

—Why do you hate your mother Steve?
—She wouldn't let go ...

Steve, despite his initial reticence, warmed up to his topic, and suddenly had plenty to say. Steve definitely hated Frances, but there were no end to his appellations against Ken. Ken was an ass, he said. He was soft. He couldn't handle it. He was dumb, just dumb.

Steve hated Ken because Ken wouldn't stand up to Frances. He didn't have any respect for Ken either, because Ken was so easy to deceive. Steve enjoyed playing games with Ken's mind.

—I make him do things, he said, things he would never do because he doesn't have the guts. Then make him forget about it later. He gets so confused. Haha ...

—What do you make Ken do?
—I make him lie. I make him hurt people.

Steve smiled, gloating over his exploits.

—Oh, I fixed him good, he went on. When he went to Los Angeles. Oh, I am so good.

\* \* \*

Salerno and Finnegan, sitting in the other room, were not impressed with what they saw as a calculated performance by a defendant to avoid punishment, and not even a good one.

But at the mention of Los Angeles their ears started flapping. Suddenly they were really paying attention. Whether or not Ken Bianchi was a true multiple personality or whether this was all an act, if Ken as "Steve" disclosed verifiable details about the murders which connected them to Buono, it would at least help them build their case against one of the two stranglers.

Steve continued:

—I was with him one night ... he walked in on his cousin, Angelo. And Angelo had a girl over ... Ken walked in—in the middle of Angelo killing this girl.

—Who's Angelo? asked Watkins.

—This turkey he knows in Los Angeles. His cousin. I made him go over to Angelo's and think all these morbid thoughts.

—Like what?

—Like there's nothing wrong with killin'. And then I make him forget about it later, see?

Salerno and Finnegan looked at each other, rolling their eyes. Salerno had diligently brought his notebook and pencil, but so far he had only made one note: "Bullshit", in capitals and underlined.

—You made him kill? Who did you make him kill?

—The girls. I made him think it was his mother and people he hated. Then I made him forget about it. I stitched that turkey up so good, haha ...

—How did Ken kill the girls?

—Uh, he killed some of 'em and he—he helped with others.

—You mean him and Angelo together?

—Yeah.

—I see. Well, how would he kill 'em? Would he shoot 'em or what?

—Oh, I made him strangle 'em all.

Dr. Watkins continued trying to get "Steve" to open about the murders—which wasn't difficult. This Steve, unlike Ken, was very forthcoming about his involvement, and particularly open about Angelo's involvement.

But Watkins wanted to bring the conversation around to Washington, since the killing of Karen and Diane was the immediate legal challenge with which Ken was faced. He asked Steve about Karen Mandic. How did Ken know Karen?

Steve explained that Ken and Karen had been friends. Steve hated anyone that Ken liked and he decided to "get even". He made Ken kill her and Diane, he said; He told Ken that it was the people who made his father go away. (Watkins knew from reviewing the clinical literature on Ken's early life that

Ken's father had died suddenly from a heart attack when Ken was in his early teens. Ken had been close to and loved his father). Steve explained that he had strangled the girls, put them in the car and driven them to a street. Ken later "woke up" to find himself walking down the road and had no memory of how he had gotten there or of the murders.

Steve also talked about Yolanda Washington. Those present surmised this, as Ken spoke of a "black girl", and Yolanda had been the only black victim in Los Angeles.

—We picked her up downtown, down in Hollywood. She was a hussy. We drove around, an' I fucked her, and she was getting more and more terrified. Angelo said, get rid of her. So I did.

Steve gave Angelo's full name as Angelo Buono. He said Angelo ran a car upholstery business in Glendale, and gave the exact address. Whether or not Ken was faking, this was useful information for the detectives. Angelo had admitted his previous association with Ken in Los Angeles, and Ken was tied by direct physical evidence to the Washington murders. The likelihood that Ken and Angelo together were the Hillside Stranglers was now looking a watertight proposition.

—You fixed Ken good, said Dr. Watkins.

—He's such a sap, said Steve, laughing. I wish I could stay out. I wanna be out!

Even though Ken was weak, he had one ace, one power over Steve. Ken trapped Steve in his body. Ken limited what Steve could do, what fun and games he could get up to.

—What would you do if you got out? asked Watkins.

—I'd kill Ken. I got to get rid of him, make him disappear.

—Who else would you kill?

—I don't know. I'd find somebody.

Dr. Watkins brought up the fact that Steve had exclusively killed women. Did he ever kill men, or want to kill men?

—Ken hates women. I mean, I hate women.

—Why?

—They hurt ...

# Chapter 25

Salerno and Finnegan were disgusted by what they had just seen. Not only had Watkins basically handed Bianchi his defense on a silver platter, but in return, the buffoon of a doctor was actually buying Ken's horseshit.

How could he not see that Bianchi was faking? It was so obvious. One thing in particular alerted the detectives that what they were seeing was pure theatre. Bianchi had at times slipped between the two identities, forgetting who was who: "Ken hates women. I mean, I hate women". It also appeared to Salerno and Finnegan that the nasty, aggressive personality "Steve", which so contrasted to all-American good boy Ken, had been consciously modeled off Angelo Buono.

To Salerno and Finnegan, Watkins' naivety, or single-minded focus on growing his professional credentials by discovery and documenting of another case of MPD—never mind that twelve women were dead—was amply demonstrated by his conduct towards Bianchi at the conclusion of the session. Watkins, having sent "Steve" away back into Ken's subconscious, spoke to the alarmed and frightened patient Ken, who denied any awareness of the alter personality, and was confused about what had just happened, having had "lost time". Watkins reassured Ken that he would learn more about "Steve" in the coming weeks, and that "Ken" would grow stronger, while "Steve" grew weaker. It would be difficult and scary, but with continued therapy and healing, Ken could reintegrate and recover these repressed and split off parts of himself, restore his full range of "thoughts, memories, dreams and so forth" until he fully understood "what had happened".

To the detectives' minds, Watkins had uncritically swallowed Bianchi's performance, taking for granted that which actually required proof. The doctor had approached Ken simply as if he were another patient, forgetting—or perhaps merely overlooking for his own professional benefit—the fact that this was a criminal investigation in which the suspect was accused of murder, with execution the possible penalty.

Meanwhile, Dr. Watkins hurried back excitedly to his desk to write up his report. He was absolutely confident that Ken was a multiple personality. As far as Watkins was concerned, Ken acted in the exact ways that multiples behaved, and he had observed many of them over the course of his professional practice, so he wasn't readily willing to doubt his own observations.

How was it possible that the cops and the psychiatrist had come to such radically different conclusions?

One explanation, the one favored by the detectives themselves, was that Dr. Watkins had overlooked Bianchi's motivations arising from the legal context of the psychiatric assessment. Bianchi had great motivation to lie, and the cops had already concluded he was a sociopath, and lying and performing is what sociopaths do best.

Another explanation is that the psychiatrist and the rest of the defense team were seeing a different evidential backdrop for their conclusions.

Dr. Watkins' report to Dean Brett, which diagnosed Ken without hesitation as a multiple personality, made clear it was not only the emergence of the alter personality "Steve" under hypnosis that convinced him, but Bianchi's background related in the clinical literature from Rochester. That history exactly fit the picture of trauma and abuse consistent with a future diagnosis.

Watkins explained to Brett that Ken's childhood exhibited several factors in common with those of other children who had gone on to develop an altered ego state through hysterical dissociation. Typically, in the family of origin, one parent is passive and one is dominant. Ken's adoptive father had often been away working when Ken was growing up, and then had died when Ken was in his crucial formative years; Frances was an overbearing "smother" who had made Ken the very focus of her existence, a burden too great for a young and sensitive boy with few other resources to fall back on.

Punishment in such a family tends to be extreme and inconsistent. One day the child is praised for a certain behavior, and another day beaten for doing the very same thing. A classic observation about punitive discipline of children and the potential therein for severe and lasting damage to the personality is the contrast between what is sometimes referred to as "positive" versus "negative" abuse. "Positive" punishment might be harsh, but if it is consistent, the damage will generally not be great. But inconsistent aggressive punishment predicts serious mental health outcomes. Children in these households are more likely to develop dissociative conditions. They are also—although this was not highlighted in Watkin's report—more likely to develop severe antisocial traits, and in the worst cases personality disorder or psychopathy.

Physical, psychological and sexual abuse in such families is typical. The individual eventually responds to this unbearable environment by "splitting", creating one or more personalities to handle the abuse on behalf of the victim. Tough-guy "Steve", Watkins opined, had probably been created by Ken as his protector. Eventually Steve channeled all the rage that Ken had felt towards his mother, and by extension, women in general. Ken, on the other hand, continued to play the part of the good son who would do anything in his power to earn his mother's approval.

A final development cemented the growing consensus amongst the defense team that Bianchi was a true dissociative. Dean Brett, in delving into Bianchi's past in Rochester, had contacted the psychologist who had written the DePaul clinic report when Ken was eleven. That particular psychologist, one Dr. Dowling, had offered the following view: "in my opinion the psychological test data from 1962 [when he was eleven] are quite consistent with a subsequent condition of multiple personality".

Watkins and Brett had spent a decent amount of time with Ken outside the formal diagnostic setting. They agreed on a certain view of Ken's character. They saw an easy-going, pleasant, friendly young man, who had absolutely no idea how he had got in such a terrible situation.

Watkins later remarked that he had observed Ken was more concerned about "what was happening inside" than the possibility of punishment. Ken didn't believe he could have committed the crimes, and for the longest time refused to allow his attorney to prepare an insanity defense. This was not the behavior of a guilty person trying to escape consequences.

While Watkins and the detectives disagreed about what had unfolded during the session, there was no doubt that the revelations were fascinating. While Bianchi was not accepting accountability for his crimes, he was confessing to them; and he had directly fingered Buono as his accomplice. At the same time, even if "Steve" was an invention, it was clear that Ken Bianchi was telling those present something true about himself, his pathology, his motivations.

"Ken" and "Steve" hated women, and sought to exact revenge on them for all the indignities inflicted by Ken's mother.

But what was the truth? Who was Ken really—the innocent man with a shattered mind, or a sociopathic murderer?

Dean Brett and a panel of psychiatrists delved into the past searching for an answer. Their difficulty was that history could have turned him out either way.

Dear reader,

We hope you enjoyed reading *A City Owned*. Please take a moment to leave a review in Amazon, even if it's a short one. Your opinion is important to us.

Discover more books by O.J. Modjeska at https://www.nextchapter.pub/authors/oj-modjeska

Want to know when one of our books is free or discounted for Kindle? Join the newsletter at http://eepurl.com/bqqB3H

Best regards,

O.J. Modjeska and the Next Chapter Team

# Books by the Author

Gone - Catastrophe In Paradise
A City Owned (Murder by Increments Book 1)
Killing Cousins (Murder by Increments Book 2)

You might also like:

Killing Cousins by O.J. Modjeska

To read first chapter for free, head to:
https://www.nextchapter.pub/books/killing-cousins

Printed in Poland
by Amazon Fulfillment
Poland Sp. z o.o., Wrocław